Anson D. F. Randolph and Company

Songs of Praise

A Selection of Standard Hymns and Tunes, for Sunday Schools and Social Meetings.

Anson D. F. Randolph and Company

Songs of Praise
A Selection of Standard Hymns and Tunes, for Sunday Schools and Social Meetings.

ISBN/EAN: 9783337089559

Printed in Europe, USA, Canada, Australia, Japan

Cover: Foto ©Thomas Meinert / pixelio.de

SONGS OF PRAISE.

A SELECTION OF STANDARD HYMNS AND TUNES.

FOR

SUNDAY-SCHOOLS AND SOCIAL MEETINGS.

NEW YORK:
ANSON D. F. RANDOLPH & COMPANY.
900 BROADWAY, COR. 20th STREET.

NOTE.

This Book has been compiled in answer to a demand for a small selection of Standard Hymns and Tunes, for use in the Sunday-school and Social meeting, and in the hope that it may serve not only the immediate purposes for which it is designed, but also to familiarize the minds of children and youth especially with some of the best and purest Hymns and Tunes of the Church. The compilers believe that the Service of Praise in the Sunday-school and Social meeting should be in harmony with that of the Church, and this has been constantly kept in mind in the preparation of this Volume.

THE TEN COMMANDMENTS.

EXODUS XX. 1-17.

GOD spake all these words, saying:

I am the Lord thy God, which have brought thee out of the land of Egypt, out of the house of bondage.

I. Thou shalt have no other gods before Me.

II. Thou shalt not make unto thee any graven image, or any likeness of any thing that is in heaven above, or that is in the earth beneath, or that is in the water under the earth: thou shalt not bow down thyself to them, nor serve them.

For I the Lord thy God am a jealous God, visiting the iniquity of the fathers upon the children unto the third and fourth generation of them that hate Me: and shewing mercy unto thousands of them that love Me, and keep My commandments.

III. Thou shalt not take the name of the Lord thy God in vain.

For the Lord will not hold him guiltless that taketh His name in vain.

IV. Remember the sabbath day, to keep it holy. Six days shalt thou labor, and do all thy work: but the seventh day is the sabbath of the Lord thy God in it thou shalt not do any work, thou, nor thy son, nor thy daughter, thy man-servant, nor thy maid-servant, nor thy cattle, nor thy stranger that is within thy gates.

For in six days the Lord made heaven and earth, the sea, and all that in them is, and rested the seventh day: wherefore the Lord blessed the sabbath day, and hallowed it.

V. Honor thy father and thy mother: that thy days may be long upon the land which the Lord thy God giveth thee.

VI. Thou shalt not kill.

VII. Thou shalt not commit adultery.

VIII. Thou shalt not steal.

IX. Thou shalt not bear false witness against thy neighbor.

X. Thou shalt not covet thy neighbor's house, thou shalt not covet thy neighbor's wife, nor his man-servant, nor his maid-servant, nor his ox, nor his ass, nor any thing that is thy neighbor's.

THE LORD'S PRAYER.

MATTHEW vi. 9-13.

OUR Father who art in heaven:

Hallowed be Thy name. Thy kingdom come. Thy will be done on earth, as it is in heaven. Give us this day our daily bread. And forgive us our debts, as we forgive our debtors. And lead us not into temptation, but deliver us from evil.

For Thine is the kingdom, and the power, and the glory, forever. Amen.

THE APOSTLES' CREED.

I BELIEVE in GOD THE FATHER Almighty, Maker of heaven and earth:

And in JESUS CHRIST His only Son our Lord; who was conceived by the Holy Ghost; born of the Virgin Mary; suffered under Pontius Pilate; was crucified, dead, and buried; He descended into hell; the third day He rose again from the dead; He ascended into heaven; and sitteth on the right hand of God the Father Almighty; from thence He shall come to judge the quick and the dead.

I believe in the HOLY GHOST; the holy Catholic Church; the Communion of Saints; the Forgiveness of sins; the Resurrection of the body; and the Life everlasting Amen.

NICAEA. 11, 12, 12, 10. **I** Rev. John Bacchus Dykes. 1861.

1. Ho - LY, ho - ly, ho - ly, Lord God Al - might - y! Ear - ly in the
morn - ing our song shall rise to Thee; Ho - ly, ho - ly, ho - ly!
Mer - ci - ful and Might - y! God in Three Per - sons, Bless-éd Trin - i - ty!

I

2 Holy, holy, holy! all the saints adore Thee,
Casting down their golden crowns around the glassy sea;
Cherubim and seraphim falling down before Thee,
Which wert, and art, and evermore shalt be.

3 Holy, holy, holy! though the darkness hide Thee,
Though the eye of sinful man Thy glory may not see,
Only Thou art holy, there is none beside Thee,
Perfect in power, in love, and purity.

4 Holy, holy, holy! Lord God Almighty!
All Thy works shall praise Thy Name, in earth, and sky, and sea;
Holy, holy, holy! Lord God Almighty!
God in Three Persons, Blesséd Trinity!

Bp. Reginald Heber. (1783—1826.) 1827.

MESSIAH. 7. D. **2** Louis J. Ferdinand Herold. (1791–1833.) 1830.
Arr. by George Kingsley. (1811—) 1838.

1. GOD e - ternal, Lord of all, Low - ly at Thy feet we fall, All the earth doth worship Thee;
We a - midst the throng would be. All the ho - ly an - gels cry, Hail, thrice ho - ly,
God most high! Lord of all the heavenly powers, Be the same loud anthem ours.

2 *"Te Deum laudamus."*

2 Glorified apostles raise
Night and day continual praise;
Hast Thou not a mission too
For Thy children here to do?
With Thy prophets' goodly line
We in mystic bond combine;
For Thou hast to babes revealed
Things that to the wise were sealed

Rev. James Elwin Millard. 1848. ab.

3 *The Shout of Triumph.*

1 SONS of Zion, raise your songs,
Praise to Zion's King belongs;
His the victor's crown and fame,
Glory to the Saviour's name.
Sore the strife, but rich the prize,
Precious in the Victor's eyes;
Glorious is the work achieved,
Satan vanquished, man relieved.

2 Sing we then the Victor's praise,
Go ye forth and strew the ways;
Bid Him welcome to His throne,
He is worthy, He alone.
Place the crown upon His brow;
Every knee to Him shall bow;
Him the brightest seraph sings,
Heaven proclaims Him "King of kings."

Rev. Thomas Kelly. (1769—1855.) 1839.

4 *Doxology.*

PRAISE our glorious King and Lord,
Angels waiting on His word,
Saints that walk with Him in white,
Pilgrims walking in His light:
Glory to the Eternal One,
Glory to His Only Son,
Glory to the Spirit be
Now, and through eternity.

Rev. Alexander Ramsay Thompson. (1822—) 1869

MARTYN. 7. D. 3 Simeon Butler Marsh. (1798—) 1834.

5

"Jesus, Lover of my Soul."

1 JESUS, Lover of my soul,
Let me to Thy bosom fly,
While the nearer waters roll,
While the tempest still is high;
Hide me, O my Saviour, hide,
Till the storm of life is past;
Safe into the haven guide;
O receive my soul at last.

2 Other refuge have I none;
Hangs my helpless soul on Thee;
Leave, ah leave me not alone,
Still support and comfort me.
All my trust on Thee is stayed,
All my help from Thee I bring;
Cover my defenceless head
With the shadow of Thy wing.

3 Wilt Thou not regard my call?
Wilt Thou not accept my prayer?
Lo, I sink, I faint, I fall!
Lo, on Thee I cast my care.
Reach me out Thy gracious hand!
While I of Thy strength receive,
Hoping against hope I stand,
Dying, and behold I live!

Rev. Charles Wesley. (1708—1788.) 1740.

6

"All I want."

1 THOU, O Christ, art all I want;
More than all in Thee I find:
Raise the fallen, cheer the faint,
Heal the sick, and lead the blind.
Just and holy is Thy Name;
I am all unrighteousness;
False and full of sin I am,
Thou art full of truth and grace.

2 Plenteous grace with Thee is found,
Grace to cover all my sin:
Let the healing streams abound,
Make and keep me pure within.
Thou of Life the Fountain art;
Freely let me take of Thee;
Spring Thou up within my heart,
Rise to all eternity.

Rev. Charles Wesley. 1740.

7

"Dignare me, O Jesu, rogo te."

1 JESUS, grant me this, I pray,
Ever in Thy heart to stay;
Let me evermore abide
Hidden in Thy wounded side.

2 If the evil one prepare,
Or the world, a tempting snare,
I am safe, when I abide
In Thy heart and wounded side.

3 If the flesh, more dangerous still,
Tempt my soul to deeds of ill,
Naught I fear, when I abide
In Thy heart and wounded side.

4 Death will come one day to me;
Jesus, cast me not from Thee:
Dying, let me still abide
In Thy heart and wounded side.

Of unknown authorship and date
Tr. by Rev. Sir Henry Williams Baker (1821—) 1861.

LENOX. H. M. 4 Jonathan Edson. 1782.

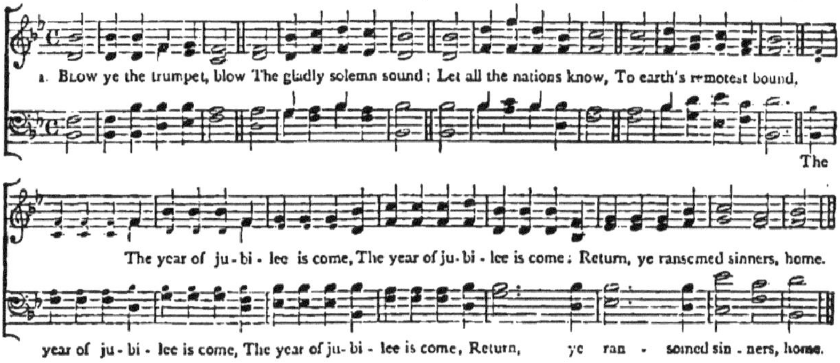
1. Blow ye the trumpet, blow The gladly solemn sound; Let all the nations know, To earth's remotest bound,
The
The year of ju-bi-lee is come, The year of ju-bi-lee is come; Return, ye ransomed sinners, home.
year of ju-bi-lee is come, The year of ju-bi-lee is come, Return, ye ran-somed sin-ners, home.

8

"The Year of Jubilee is come."

2 Jesus, our great High-Priest,
  Hath full atonement made:
Ye weary Spirits, rest,
  Ye mournful souls, be glad;
The year of jubilee is come;
Return, ye ransomed sinners, home.

3 Extol the Lamb of God,
  The all-atoning Lamb
Redemption in His blood
  Throughout the world proclaim:
The year of jubilee is come;
Return, ye ransomed sinners, home.

4 The gospel trumpet hear,
  The news of heavenly grace;
And, saved from earth, appear
  Before your Saviour's face:
The year of jubilee is come;
Return, ye ransomed sinners, home.

Rev. Charles Wesley. (1708—1788.) 1750

9

Captivity led captive.
Ps. lxviii. 18. Eph. iv. 8.

1 The happy morn is come;
  The Saviour leaves the grave;
His glorious work is done,
  Almighty now to save:
Captivity is captive led,
Since Jesus liveth that was dead.

2 Who to our charge shall lay
  Iniquity and guilt?
All sin is done away,
  Since His rich blood was spilt,
Captivity is captive led,
Since Jesus liveth that was dead.

3 Christ hath the ransom paid;
  The glorious work is done;
On Him our help is laid,
  The victory is won.
Captivity is captive led,
Since Jesus liveth that was dead.

4 Hail the triumphant Lord!
  The resurrection Thou!
We bless Thy sacred word,
  Before Thy throne we bow:
Captivity is captive led,
Since Jesus liveth that was dead.

Rev. Thomas Haweis. (1732—1820.) 1792. ab.

1. To Him that chose us first Be - fore the world be - gan ; To Him that bore the curse To
save rebellious man ; To Him that formed our hearts a-new, Is end-less praise and glo - ry due.

10

Praise to the Trinity.

1 To Him that chose us first
Before the world began ;
To Him that bore the curse
To save rebellious man ;
To Him that formed | Is endless praise
Our hearts anew, | And glory due.

2 The Father's love shall run
Through our immortal songs ;
We bring to God the Son
Hosannas on our tongues :
Our lips address | With equal praise,
The Spirit's name | And zeal the same.

3 Let every saint above,
And angels round the throne,
Forever bless and love
The sacred Three in One :
Thus heaven shall raise | When earth and time
His honors high, | Grow old and die.

Rev. Isaac Watts. 1709.

11

DOXOLOGY.

To God the Father's throne
Perpetual honors raise ;
Glory to God the Son,
To God the Spirit praise :
And while our lips | Our faith adores
Their tributes bring, | The name we sing.

Rev. Isaac Watts. 1709.

12

God our Preserver.

Ps. cxxi.

1 UPWARD I lift mine eyes,
From God is all my aid ;
The God that built the skies,
And earth and nature made :
God is the tower | His grace is nigh
To which I fly ; | In every hour.

2 My feet shall never slide,
And fall in fatal snares,
Since God, my guard and guide,
Defends me from my fears :
Those wakeful eyes, | Shall Israel keep
That never sleep, | When dangers rise.

3 No burning heats by day,
Nor blasts of evening air,
Shall take my health away,
If God be with me there :
Thou art my sun, | To guard my head
And Thou my shade, | By night or noon.

4 Hast Thou not given Thy word
To save my soul from death ?
And I can trust my Lord
To keep my mortal breath :
I'll go and come, | Till from on high
Nor fear to die, | Thou call me home.

Rev. Isaac Watts. 1719.

ITALIAN HYMN. 6, 4. **6** Felice Giardini. (1716—1796.) 1760.

1. COME, Thou al - might - y King, Help us Thy Name to sing, Help us to praise:
Father all - glo - rious, O'er all vic - to - rious, Come, and reign o - ver us, Ancient of days.

13 *The Trinity invoked.*

2 Jesus, our Lord, arise;
Scatter our enemies,
And make them fall:
Let Thine almighty aid
Our sure defence be made;
Our souls on Thee be stayed;
Lord, hear our call.

3 Come, Thou Incarnate Word,
Gird on Thy mighty sword,
Our prayer attend:
Come, and Thy people bless,
And give Thy Word success
Spirit of holiness,
On us descend.

4 Come, Holy Comforter,
Thy sacred witness bear
In this glad hour:
Thou who Almighty art,
Now rule in every heart,
And ne'er from us depart,
Spirit of power.

5 To the great One and Three
Eternal praises be
Hence, evermore.
His sovereign majesty
May we in glory see,
And to eternity
Love and adore.

Rev. Charles Wesley. (1708—1788.) 1757.

14 *"Speed on Thy Word."*

1 LORD of all power and might,
Father of love and light,
Speed on Thy word:
O let the gospel sound
All the wide world around,
Wherever man is found:
God speed His word.

2 Hail, blessed Jubilee:
Thine, Lord, the glory be;
Forevermore!
Thine was the mighty plan,
From Thee the work began;
Away with praise of man,
Glory to God!

3 Lo, what embattled foes,
Stern in their hate, oppose
God's holy word:
One for His truth we stand,
Strong in His own right hand,
Firm as a martyr-band:
God shield His word.

4 Onward shall be our course,
Despite of fraud or force;
God is before:
His word ere long shall run
Free as the noon-day sun;
His purpose must be done:
God bless His word.

Rev. Hugh Stowell. (1799—1865.) 1854. al. alt

OLD HUNDRED. L. M. Guillaume Franck. 1545.

1. ALL peo - ple that on earth do dwell, Sing to the Lord with cheerful voice:
Him serve with fear, His praise forth tell, Come ye be - fore Him, and re - joice.

15 *All People summoned to worship.*

Ps. c.

2 The Lord, ye know is God indeed,
Without our aid He did us make;
We are His flock, He doth us feed,
And for His sheep He doth us take.

3 O enter then His gates with praise,
Approach with joy His courts unto:
Praise, laud, and bless His name always,
For it is seemly so to do.

4 For why? the Lord our God is good,
His mercy is forever sure:
His truth at all times firmly stood,
And shall from age to age endure.

Rev. William Kethe. 1561.

16 *Praise from all Nations.*

Ps. cxvii.

1 FROM all that dwell below the skies,
Let the Creator's praise arise:
Let the Redeemer's name be sung
Through every land, by every tongue.

2 Eternal are Thy mercies, Lord;
Eternal truth attends Thy word;
Thy praise shall sound from shore to shore
Till suns shall rise and set no more.

Rev. Isaac Watts. 1719.

17 *Grateful Adoration.*

Ps. c.

1 BEFORE Jehovah's awful throne,
Ye nations, bow with sacred joy;
Know that the Lord is God alone;
He can create, and He destroy.

2 His sovereign power, without our aid,
Made us of clay, and formed us men;
And when, like wand'ring sheep, we strayed,
He brought us to His fold again.

3 We'll crowd Thy gates with thankful songs,
High as the heavens our voices raise;
And earth, with her ten thousand tongues,
Shall fill Thy courts with sounding praise.

4 Wide as the world is Thy command,
Vast as eternity Thy love;
Firm as a rock Thy truth must stand,
When rolling years shall cease to move

Rev. Isaac Watts. (1674—1748.) 1719. ab. and alt
Rev. John Wesley. 1703--1791. 1741.

SOLNEY. (WORTHING.) 8, 7. Johann A. P. Schulz. (1747—1800.)

1. PRAISE the Lord, ye heavens, a - dore him; Praise Him, an - gels, in the height;
Sun and moon, re - joice be - fore Him; Praise Him, all ye stars and light.

18

Praise from the whole Creation.

Ps. cxlviii.

2 Praise the Lord, for He hath spoken;
   Worlds His mighty voice obeyed;
Laws which never shall be broken,
   For their guidance He hath made.

3 Praise the Lord, for He is glorious;
   Never shall His promise fail;
God hath made His saints victorious;
   Sin and death shall not prevail.

4 Praise the God of our salvation;
   Hosts on high, His power proclaim;
Heaven and earth, and all creation,
   Laud and magnify His name.

Rev. John Kempthorne. (1775—1838.) 1809.

19

Praise on Earth and in Heaven.

Rev. iv. 11.

1 PRAISE to Thee, Thou great Creator,
   Praise be Thine from every tongue;
Join, my soul, with every creature,
   Join the universal song.

2 Father, Source of all compassion,
   Pure unbounded grace is Thine:
Hail the God of our salvation,
   Praise Him for His love divine.

3 For ten thousand blessings given,
   For the richest gifts bestowed,
Sound His praise through earth and heaven,
   Sound Jehovah's praise aloud.

4 Joyfully on earth adore Him,
   Till in Heaven our song we raise;
There, enraptured fall before Him,
   Lost in wonder, love, and praise.

Rev. John Fawcett. (1739—1817.) 1767. alt.

20

DOXOLOGY.

WORSHIP, honor, glory, blessing,
   Lord, we offer to Thy name:
Young and old their praise expressing,
   Join Thy goodness to proclaim.
As the saints in Heaven adore Thee,
   We would bow before Thy throne;
As the angels serve before Thee,
   So on earth Thy will be done!

Edward Osler. (1798—1863.) 1836.

LYONS 10, 11. 9 Francis Joseph Haydn. (1732—1809.) 1770.

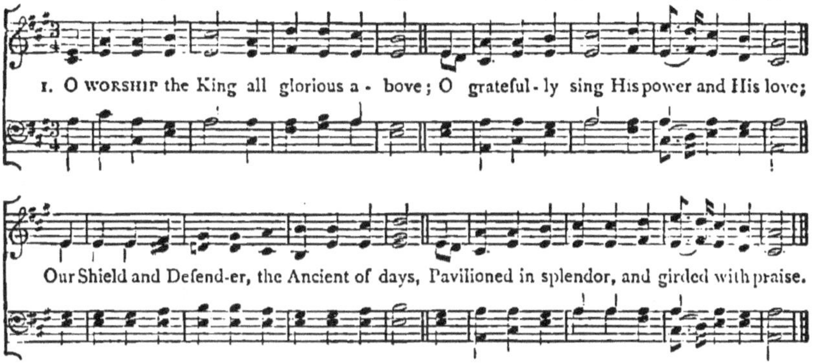
1. O WORSHIP the King all glorious a - bove; O grateful - ly sing His power and His love;
Our Shield and Defend-er, the Ancient of days, Pavilioned in splendor, and girded with praise.

21 *The Majesty and Mercy of God.*

Ps. civ.

2 O tell of His might, O sing of His grace,
Whose robe is the light, whose canopy space;
His chariots of wrath deep thunder clouds form,
And dark is His path on the wings of the storm.

3 Thy bountiful care what tongue can recite?
It breathes in the air, it shines in the light,
It streams from the hills, it descends to the plain,
And sweetly distils in the dew and the rain.

4 Frail children of dust, and feeble as frail,
In Thee do we trust, nor find Thee to fail:
Thy mercies how tender, how firm to the end,
Our Maker, Defender, Redeemer, and Friend.

5 O measureless Might, ineffable Love,
While angels delight to hymn Thee above,
The humbler creation, though feeble their lays,
With true adoration shall lisp to Thy praise.

Sir Robert Grant. (1785—1838.) 1839.

22 *He rules over all.*

1 YE servants of God, your Master proclaim,
And publish abroad His wonderful Name;
The Name all-victorious of Jesus extol;
His kingdom is glorious, and rules over all.

2 God ruleth on high, almighty to save;
And still He is nigh, His presence we have;
The great congregation His triumph shall sing,
Ascribing salvation to Jesus our King.

3 "Salvation to God who sits on the throne,"
Let all cry aloud, and honor the Son;
The praises of Jesus the angels proclaim,
Fall down on their faces, and worship the Lamb.

4 Then let us adore, and give Him His right;
All glory and power, and wisdom and might;
All honor and blessing, with angels above,
And thanks never ceasing, and infinite love.

Rev. Charles Wesley. (1708—1788.) 1744. ab.

SILVER STREET. *S. M.* 10 Isaac Smith. 1770.

1. GRACE, 'tis a charm - ing sound, Har - mo - nious to mine ear; Heaven
with the ech - o shall re - sound, And all.... the earth shall hear.

23

Saving Grace.

Eph. ii. 5.

2 Grace first contrived a way
To save rebellious man,
And all the steps that grace display,
Which drew the wondrous plan.

3 Grace taught my wandering feet
To tread the heavenly road;
And new supplies each hour I meet,
While pressing on to God.

4 Grace all the work shall crown,
Through everlasting days;
It lays in heaven the topmost stone,
And well deserves the praise.

Rev. Philip Doddridge. (1702—1751.) 1755.

24

"The Song of Moses and the Lamb."

Rev. xv. 3.

1 AWAKE, and sing the song
Of Moses and the Lamb;
Wake every heart and every tongue,
To praise the Saviour's name.

2 Sing of His dying love;
Sing of His rising power;
Sing how He intercedes above
For those whose sins He bore.

3 Soon shall ye hear Him say,
"Ye blessed children, come;"
Soon will He call you hence away,
And take His wanderers home.

4 There shall our raptured tongue
His endless praise proclaim,
And sweeter voices swell the song
Of Moses and the Lamb.

Rev. William Hammond. (—1783.) 1745. ab. and alt.
Rev. Martin Madan. (1726—1790.) 1760. First 5 vs.

25

"Sweet is Thy Mercy."

Ps. cix. 20.

1 SWEET is Thy mercy, Lord;
Before Thy mercy-seat
My soul, adoring, pleads Thy word,
And owns Thy mercy sweet.

2 Where'er Thy name is blest,
Where'er Thy people meet,
There I delight in Thee to rest,
And find Thy mercy sweet.

3 Light Thou my weary way,
Place Thou my weary feet,
That while I stray on earth I may
Still find Thy mercy sweet.

4 Thus shall the heavenly host
Hear all my songs repeat
To Father, Son, and Holy Ghost,
My joy, Thy mercy sweet.

Rev. John Samuel Bewley Monsell. (1811—) 1862. ab.

ST. THOMAS. S. M. William Tansur. (1699—1774.) 1743.

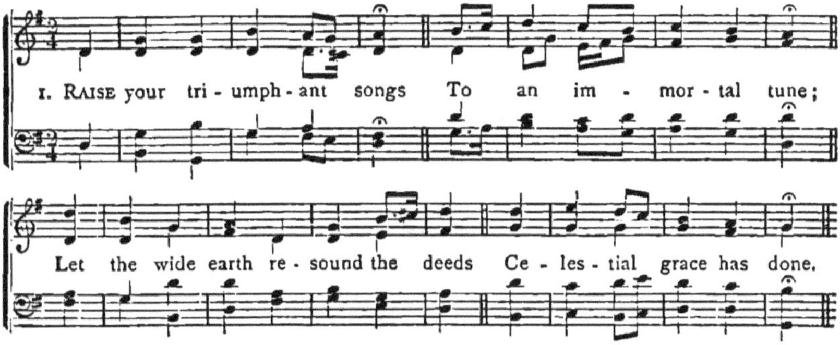
1. RAISE your tri - umph - ant songs To an im - mor - tal tune;
Let the wide earth re - sound the deeds Ce - les - tial grace has done.

26

Christ sent to save us.

2 Sing how Eternal Love
Its chief belovèd chose,
And bade Him raise our wretched race
From their abyss of woes.

3 'Twas mercy filled the throne,
And wrath stood silent by,
When Christ was sent with pardons down
To rebels doomed to die.

4 Now, sinners, dry your tears,
Let hopeless sorrow cease;
Bow to the sceptre of His love,
And take the offered peace.

5 Lord, we obey Thy call;
We lay a humble claim
To the salvation Thou hast brought,
And love and praise Thy name.

Rev. Isaac Watts. (1674—1748.) 1709. ab.

27

"Bless the Lord."
Neh. ix. 5.

1 STAND up, and bless the Lord,
Ye people of His choice;
Stand up, and bless the Lord your God,
With heart, and soul, and voice.

2 O, for the living flame,
From his own altar brought,
To touch our lips, our minds inspire,
And wing to heaven our thought.

3 God is our strength and song,
And His salvation ours;
Then be His love in Christ proclaimed
With all our ransomed powers.

4 Stand up, and bless the Lord,
The Lord your God adore;
Stand up, and bless His glorious name
Henceforth for evermore.

James Montgomery. (1771—1854.) 1825. ab

ST. GERVAIS. 7. **12** Arr. by Rev. William Henry Havergal. (1793—1870.)

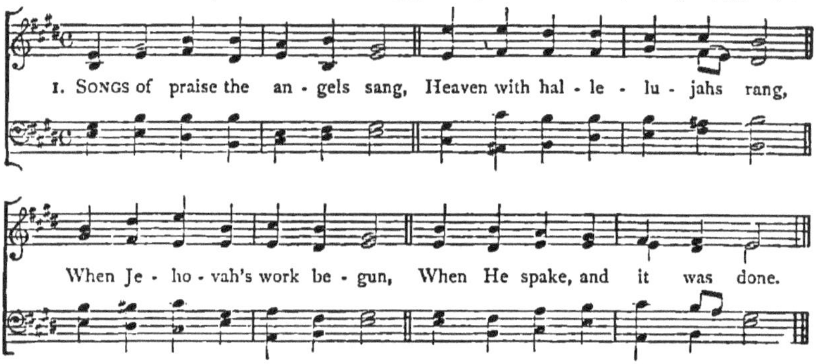
1. SONGS of praise the an - gels sang, Heaven with hal - le - lu - jahs rang,
When Je - ho - vah's work be - gun, When He spake, and it was done.

28

"Glory to God in the highest."

Luke ii. 13.

2 Songs of praise awoke the morn,
When the Prince of Peace was born;
Songs of praise arose, when He
Captive led captivity.

3 Heaven and earth must pass away,
Songs of praise shall crown that day;
God will make new heavens, new earth,
Songs of praise shall hail their birth.

4 And can man alone be dumb
Till that glorious kingdom come?
No; the Church delights to raise
Psalms, and hymns, and songs of praise.

5 Saints below, with heart and voice,
Still in songs of praise rejoice;
Learning here, by faith and love,
Songs of praise to sing above.

James Montgomery. (1771—1854.) 1819, 1853.

29

"Hail, celestial Goodness, hail."

1 HOLY, holy, holy Lord,
Be Thy glorious name adored:
Lord, Thy mercies never fail;
Hail, celestial Goodness, hail!

2 Though unworthy, Lord, Thine ear,
Deign our humble songs to hear;
Purer praise we hope to bring,
When around Thy throne we sing.

3 While on earth ordained to stay,
Guide our footsteps in Thy way,
Till we come to dwell with Thee,
Till we all Thy glory see.

4 Then with angel-harps again
We will wake a nobler strain;
There, in joyful songs of praise,
Our triumphant voices raise.

5 There no tongue shall silent be,
All shall join in harmony;
That through heaven's capacious round
Praise to Thee may ever sound.

Rev. Benjamin Williams. 1778.

NURUMBERG. 7. **13** Johann Rudolf Ahle. (1625—1673.) 1664.

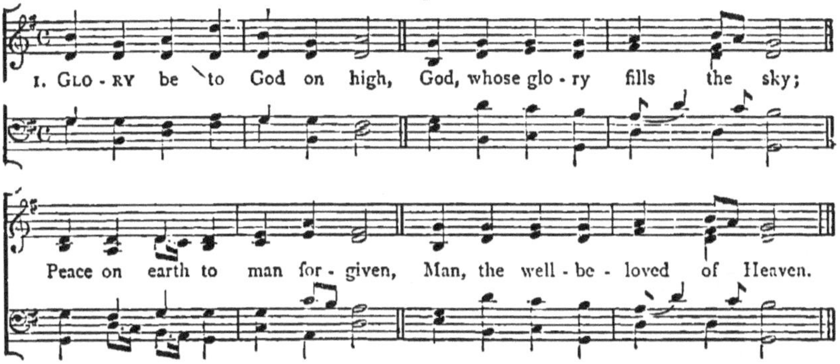
1. GLO - RY be to God on high, God, whose glo - ry fills the sky;
Peace on earth to man for - given, Man, the well - be - loved of Heaven.

30 *"Gloria in Excelsis."*

2 Sovereign Father, heavenly King,
Thee we now presume to sing;
Glad, Thine attributes confess,
Glorious all, and numberless.

3 Hail, by all Thy works adored,
Hail, the everlasting Lord:
Thee, with thankful hearts we prove
God of power, and God of love.

4 Christ our Lord and God we own
Christ, the Father's Only Son;
Lamb of God, for sinners slain,
Saviour of offending man.

5 Bow Thine ear, in mercy bow;
Hear, the world's Atonement Thou:
Jesus, in Thy name we pray,
Take, O take our sins away.

6 Hear, for Thou, O Christ, alone
Art with Thy great Father One;
One, the Holy Ghost with Thee;
One supreme, eternal Three.

Rev. Charles Wesley. (1708—1788.) 1739. ab.

31 *Praise from all.*
Ps. cxvii.

1 ALL ye Gentiles, praise the Lord,
All ye lands, your voices raise;
Heaven and earth, with loud accord,
Praise the Lord, forever praise.

2 For His truth and mercy stand,
Past, and present, and to be,
Like the years of His right hand,
Like His own eternity.

3 Praise Him, ye who know His love;
Praise Him, from the depths beneath;
Praise Him in the heights above;
Praise your Maker, all that breathe.

James Montgomery. 1822.

32 *Rejoicing on our Way.*

1 CHILDREN of the Heavenly King,
As ye journey, sweetly sing;
Sing your Saviour's worthy praise,
Glorious in His works and ways.

2 Shout, ye little flock, and blest,
You on Jesus' throne shall rest;
There your seat is now prepared,
There your kingdom and reward.

3 Fear not, brethren, joyful stand
On the borders of your land;
Jesus Christ, your Father's Son,
Bids you undismayed go on.

4 Lord, obediently we go,
Gladly leaving all below;
Only Thou our Leader be,
And we still will follow Thee.

Rev. John Cennick. (1717—1755.) 1741. ab.

HENDON. 7. Rev. C. H. Abraham Malan. (1787—1864.) 1830.

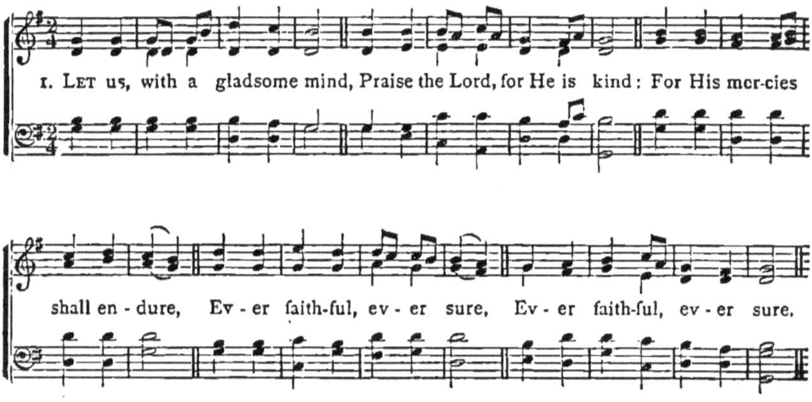
1. LET us, with a gladsome mind, Praise the Lord, for He is kind: For His mer-cies
shall en - dure, Ev - er faith-ful, ev - er sure, Ev - er faith-ful, ev - er sure.

33 *Wonders of Creation, Providence, and Grace.*

Ps. cxxxvi.

2 He, with all-commanding might,
Filled the new-made world with light:
For His mercies shall endure,
Ever faithful, ever sure.

3 All things living He doth feed,
His full hand supplies their need:
For His mercies shall endure,
Ever faithful, ever sure.

John Milton. (1608—1674.) 1624. ab. and alt.

34 *A Day in the Lord's Courts.*

1 To Thy temple I repair;
Lord, I love to worship there;
When within the veil I meet
Christ before the mercy-seat.

2 While Thy glorious praise is sung,
Touch my lips, unloose my tongue,
That my joyful soul may bless
Thee, the Lord my Righteousness.

3 While the prayers of saints ascend,
God of love, to mine attend;
Hear me, for Thy Spirit pleads,
Hear, for Jesus intercedes.

4 From Thy house when I return,
May my heart within me burn;
And at evening let me say,
"I have walked with God to-day."

James Montgomery. (1771—1854.) 1825. ab

35 *"Loving Him who first loved me."*

1 SAVIOUR, teach me day by day,
Love's sweet lesson to obey;
Sweeter lesson cannot be,
Loving Him who first loved me.

2 Teach me all Thy steps to trace,
Strong to follow in Thy grace:
Learning how to love from Thee,
Loving Him who first loved me.

Unknown Author. 1854. ab.

DENNIS. S. M. **15** Hans Georg Naegeli. (1768—1836.) 1832.
Arr. by W. B. Bradbury. (1816—1868.) 1849.

1. THE Lord my Shep - herd is; I shall be well sup - plied:
Since He is mine, and I am His, What can I want be - side?

36

The Lord our Shepherd.

Ps. xxiii.

2 He leads me to the place
  Where heavenly pasture grows;
Where living waters gently pass,
  And full salvation flows.

3 If e'er I go astray,
  He doth my soul reclaim;
And guides me, in His own right way,
  For His most holy name.

4 While He affords His aid,
  I cannot yield to fear;
Tho' I should walk thro' death's dark shade,
  My Shepherd's with me there.

5 The bounties of Thy love
  Shall crown my following days;
Nor from Thy house will I remove,
  Nor cease to speak Thy praise.

Rev. Isaac Watts. (1674—1748.) 1719.

37

The Heavenly Shepherd.

Ps. xxiii.

1 WHILE my Redeemer's near,
  My Shepherd and my Guide,
I bid farewell to anxious fear;
  My wants are all supplied.

2 To ever fragrant meads,
  Where rich abundance grows,
His gracious hand indulgent leads,
  And guards my sweet repose.

3 Dear Shepherd, if I stray,
  My wandering feet restore;
To Thy fair pastures guide my way,
  And let me rove no more.

4 Unworthy, as I am,
  Of Thy protecting care,
Jesus, I plead Thy gracious name,
  For all my hopes are there.

Miss Anne Steele. (1717—1778.) 1760. ab

BOYLSTON. S. M. Lowell Mason. (1792—1872.) 1832.

1. Blest be the tie that binds Our hearts in Chris-tian love: The
fel-low-ship of kin-dred minds Is like to that a-bove.

38

Brotherly Love.

2 Before our Father's throne
 We pour our ardent prayers;
Our fears, our hopes, our aims are one,
 Our comforts and our cares.

3 We share our mutual woes;
 Our mutual burdens bear;
And often for each other flows
 The sympathizing tear.

Rev. John Fawcett. (1739—1817.) 1772.

39

He knoweth our Frame."
Ps. ciii. 13—18.

1 The pity of the Lord
 To those that fear His name,
Is such as tender parents feel:
 He knows our feeble frame.

2 He knows we are but dust,
 Scattered with every breath
His anger, like a rising wind,
 Can send us swift to death.

3 Our days are as the grass,
 Or like the morning flower;
If one sharp blast sweep o'er the field,
 It withers in an hour.

4 But Thy compassions, Lord,
 To endless years endure;
And children's children ever find
 Thy words of promise sure.

Rev. Isaac Watts. 1719.

40

Tears of Penitence.

1 Did Christ o'er sinners weep,
 And shall our cheeks be dry?
Let floods of penitential grief
 Burst forth from every eye.

2 The Son of God in tears
 Angels with wonder see:
Be thou astonished, O my soul,
 He shed those tears for thee.

3 He wept that we might weep;
 Each sin demands a tear;
In heaven alone no sin is found,
 And there's no weeping there.

Rev. Benjamin Beddome. (1717—1795.) 1787.

DOWNS. C. M. Lowell Mason. (1792—1872.) 1832.

1. WHEN all Thy mer - cies, O my God, My ris - ing soul sur - veys,
Tran - sported with the view, I'm lost In won - der, love, and praise.

41

Mercies of God recounted.

2 Unnumbered comforts to my soul
  Thy tender care bestowed,
Before my infant heart conceived
  From whom those comforts flowed.

3 When worn with sickness, oft hast Thou
  With health renewed my face;
And, when in sins and sorrows sunk,
  Revived my soul with grace.

4 Ten thousand thousand precious gifts
  My daily thanks employ;
Nor is the least a cheerful heart
  That tastes those gifts with joy.

5 Through every period of my life
  Thy goodness I'll pursue;
And after death, in distant worlds,
  The glorious theme renew.

6 Through all eternity to Thee
  A joyful song I'll raise;
For O, eternity's too short
  To utter all Thy praise.

Joseph Addison. (1672—1719.) 1712. ab.

42

Omnipresence and Omniscience of God.

Ps. cxxxix.

1 JEHOVAH, God, Thy gracious power
  On every hand we see;
O may the blessings of each hour
  Lead all our thoughts to Thee.

2 If on the wings of morn we speed
  To earth's remotest bound,
Thy hand will there our footsteps lead,
  Thy love our path surround.

3 Thy power is in the ocean deeps,
  And reaches to the skies;
Thine eye of mercy never sleeps,
  Thy goodness never dies.

4 From morn till noon, till latest eve,
  Thy hand, O God, we see;
And all the blessings we receive,
  Proceed alone from Thee.

5 In all the varying scenes of time,
  On Thee our hopes depend;
Through every age, in every clime,
  Our Father, and our Friend.

Rev. John Thomson. (1782—1818.) 1812.

WARD. L. M.

Old Scotch Melody.
Arr. by Lowell Mason. (1792—1872.) 1830.

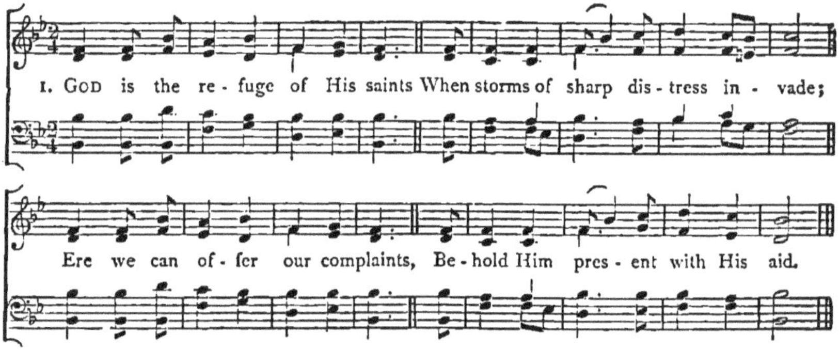
1. God is the re - fuge of His saints When storms of sharp dis - tress in - vade;
Ere we can of - fer our complaints, Be - hold Him pres - ent with His aid.

43

Safety and Triumph of God's People.

Ps. xlvi.

2 There is a stream, whose gentle flow
Supplies the city of our God,
Life, love, and joy, still gliding through,
And watering our divine abode.

3 That sacred stream, Thine holy word,
Our grief allays, our fear controls;
Sweet peace Thy promises afford,
And give new strength to fainting souls.

4 Zion enjoys her monarch's love,
Secure against a threatening hour;
Nor can her firm foundations move,
Built on His truth, and armed with power.

Rev. Isaac Watts. 1719. alt. 2l. 5v.

44

Trust in God.

Ps. xviii.

1 No change of times shall ever shock
My firm affection, Lord, to Thee;
For Thou hast always been my rock,
A fortress and defence to me.

2 Thou my deliverer art, my God;
My trust is in Thy mighty power:
Thou art my shield from foes abroad,
At home my safeguard and my tower.

3 To Thee I will address my prayer,
To whom all praise we justly owe;
So shall I, by Thy watchful care,
Be guarded from my treacherous foe.

4 Let the eternal Lord be praised,
The rock on whose defence I rest:
O'er highest heavens His name be raised
Who me with His salvation blest.

5 To Heaven I made my mournful prayer,
To God addressed my humble moan,
Who graciously inclined His ear,
And heard me from His lofty throne.

Tate and Brady. 1696. ab

45

At Dismission.

1 Dismiss us with Thy blessing, Lord;
Help us to feed upon Thy word;
All that has been amiss forgive,
And let Thy truth within us live.

2 Though we are guilty, Thou art good;
Wash all our works in Jesus' blood:
Give every fettered soul release,
And bid us all depart in peace.

Rev Joseph Hart. (1712—1768.) 1762

ANTIOCH. C. M. 19 From George Frederick Handel.
Arr. by Lowell Mason. (1792—1872.) 1836.

1. Joy to the world, the Lord is come: Let earth receive her King; Let ev - ery heart pre- pare Him room,
And heaven and na - ture sing,
And heaven and nature sing,.. And heaven,
sing,
And heaven and nature sing.
And heaven and nature sing,
And heaven and nature sing,

46 *"Joy to the World."*

Ps. xcviii.

2 Joy to the earth, the Saviour reigns:
Let men their songs employ; [plains,
While fields and floods, rocks, hills, and
Repeat the sounding joy.

3 No more let sins and sorrows grow,
Nor thorns infest the ground:
He comes to make His blessings flow
Far as the curse is found.

4 He rules the world with truth and grace,
And makes the nations prove
The glories of His righteousness,
And wonders of His love.

Rev. Isaac Watts. (1674—1748.) 1719.

47 *The Saviour's Errand.*

Is. lxi.

1 Hark, the glad sound, the Saviour comes,
The Saviour promised long;
Let every heart prepare a throne,
And every voice a song.

2 He comes, the prisoners to release
In Satan's bondage held;
The gates of brass before Him burst,
The iron fetters yield.

3 He comes, from thickest films of vice,
To clear the mental ray,
And on the eyeballs of the blind
To pour celestial day.

4 He comes, the broken heart to bind,
The bleeding soul to cure,
And with the treasures of His grace
To enrich the humble poor.

5 Our glad hosannas, Prince of Peace,
Thy welcome shall proclaim,
And heaven's eternal arches ring
With Thy beloved name.

Rev. Philip Doddridge. (1702—1751.) 173[illegible].

ZERAH. C. M. Lowell Mason. 1837.

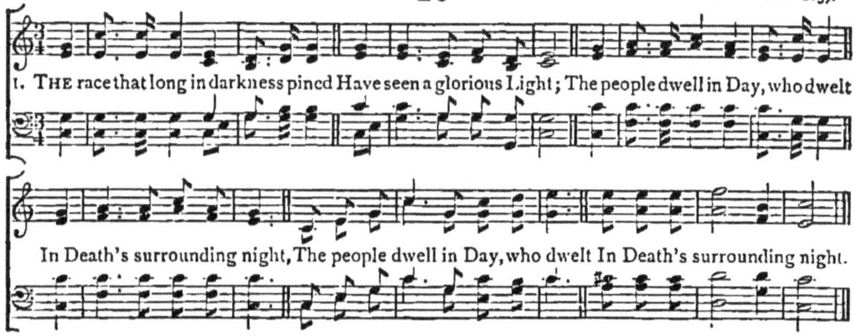
1. THE race that long in darkness pined Have seen a glorious Light; The people dwell in Day, who dwelt
In Death's surrounding night, The people dwell in Day, who dwelt In Death's surrounding night.

48

The Messiah's Coming and Kingdom.
Is. ix. 1—7.

2 To us a Child of Hope is born,
To us a Son is given;
Him shall the tribes of earth obey,
Him all the hosts of heaven.

3 His name shall be the Prince of Peace,
Forevermore adored,
The Wonderful, the Counsellor,
The great and mighty Lord.

4 His power increasing still shall spread,
His reign no end shall know:
Justice shall guard His throne above,
And Peace abound below.

Rev. John Morrison. (1749—1798.) 1770.

49

Song of the Angels.
Luke ii. 7—15.

1 WHILE shepherds watched their flocks by [night,
All seated on the ground,
The angel of the Lord came down,
And glory shone around.

2 "Fear not," said he, for mighty dread
Had seized their troubled mind;
"Glad tidings of great joy I bring
To you and all mankind.

3 "To you, in David's town, this day,
Is born of David's line,
The Saviour, who is Christ, the Lord;
And this shall be the sign:

4 "The heavenly babe you there shall find
To human view displayed,
All meanly wrapped in swathing bands,
And in a manger laid."

5 Thus spake the seraph, and forthwith
Appeared a shining throng
Of angels, praising God, and thus
Addressed their joyful song:

6 "All glory be to God on high,
And to the earth be peace;
Good-will henceforth from heaven to men
Begin, and never cease."

Tate and Brady's Supplement. 1703.

50

The Nativity of Christ.

1 MORTALS, awake, with angels join,
And chant the solemn lay;
Joy, love, and gratitude combine
To hail the auspicious day.

2 In heaven the rapturous song began,
And sweet seraphic fire
Through all the shining regions ran,
And strung and tuned the lyre.

3 Swift through the vast expanse it flew,
And loud the echo rolled;
The theme, the song, the joy, was new,
'Twas more than heaven could hold.

Rev. Samuel Medley. (1738—799.) 1800. ab.

CAROL. C. M. **21** Richard Storrs Willis. (1819—)

1. It came up - on the mid - night clear, That glo - rious song of old,
From an - gels bend - ing near the earth, To touch their harps of gold:
"Peace on the earth, good - will to men From heaven's all - gra - cious King."
The world in sol - emn still - ness lay To hear the an - gels sing.

51 *Christmas Carol.*

2 Still through the cloven skies they come,
With peaceful wings unfurled;
And still their heavenly music floats
O'er all the weary world:
Above its sad and lowly plains
They bend on hovering wing,
And ever o'er its Babel sounds
The blessèd angels sing.

3 But with the woes of sin and strife
The world has suffered long;
Beneat ι the angel-strain have rolled
Two thousand years of wrong;
And man, at war with man, hears not
The love song which they bring:
O hush the noise, ye men of strife,
And hear the angels sing.

4 For lo, the days are hastening on
By prophet bards foretold,
When with the ever circling years
Comes round the age of gold:
When Peace shall over all the earth
Its ancient splendors fling,
And the whole world give back the song
Which now the angels sing.

Rev. Edmund Hamilton Sears. (1810—). 1850.

REGENT SQUARE. 8, 7. Henry Smart. 1867

1. HARK, what mean those holy voices, Sweetly warbling in the skies? Sure th' angelic host re - joices,
Loudest hal-le - lu-jahs rise, Sure th' angelic host re-joices, Loudest hal-le-lu-jahs rise.

52

Song of the Angels.

2 Listen to the wondrous story,
Which they chant in hymns of joy:
"Glory in the highest, glory,
Glory be to God most high.

3 "Peace on earth, good-will from heaven,
Reaching far as man is found;
Souls redeemed, and sins forgiven,
Loud our golden harps shall sound.

4 "Christ is born, the great Anointed;
Heaven and earth His glory sing:
Glad receive whom God appointed
For your Prophet, Priest, and King."

5 Let us learn the wondrous story
Of our great Redeemer's birth,
Spread the brightness of His glory,
Till it cover all the earth.

Rev. John Cawood. (1775—1852.) 1819.

53

Glory to God.
1 Tim. i. 17.

1 GLORY be to God the Father,
Glory be to God the Son,
Glory be to God the Spirit,
Great Jehovah, Three in One:
Glory, glory, glory, glory,
While eternal ages run!

2 Glory be to Him who loved us,
Washed us from each spot and stain;
Glory be to Him who bought us,
Made us kings with Him to reign:
Glory, glory, glory, glory,
To the Lamb that once was slain!

3 Glory to the King of angels,
Glory to the Church's King,
Glory to the King of nations,
Heaven and earth, your praises bring:
Glory, glory, glory, glory,
To the King of glory bring!

4 Glory, blessing, praise eternal!
Thus the choir of angels sings;
Honor, riches, power, dominion!
Thus its praise creation brings:
Glory, glory, glory, glory,
Glory to the King of kings!

Rev. Horatius Bonar. (1808—) 1866

HERALD ANGELS. 7, D. 23 Felix Mendelssohn-Bartholdy. (1809—1847.) 1846

1. Hark, the herald angels sing, "Glory to the new-born King! Peace on earth, and mercy mild,
God and sinners re-conciled!" Joy-ful, all ye nations, rise,
Join the triumph of the skies; U - ni - ver-sal na- ture say,
"Christ the Lord is born to-day," U - ni - ver- sal nature say, "Christ the Lord is born to-day."

54

"Christ the Lord is born To-day."

2 Christ, by highest heaven adored,
Christ the everlasting Lord!
Late in time behold Him come,
Offspring of a Virgin's womb!
Veiled in flesh the Godhead see,
Hail, the incarnate Deity!
Pleased as Man with men to dwell,
Jesus, our Immanuel.

3 Hail the heavenly Prince of Peace!
Hail, the Sun of Righteousness!
Light and life to all He brings,
Risen with healing in His wings.
Mild He lays His glory by,
Born that man no more may die,
Born to raise the sons of earth,
Born to give them second birth.

55

The Coming of the Messiah.

Is. ix. 6.

1 Hail, all hail the joyful morn!
Tell it forth from earth to heaven,
That "to us a Child is born,"
That "to us a Son is given."

2 Angels bending from the sky,
Chanted at the wondrous birth,
"Glory be to God on high,
Peace, good-will to man on earth."

3 Him prophetic strains proclaim
King of kings, the Incarnate Word,
Great and wonderful His name,
Prince of Peace, the Mighty God.

4 Join we then our feeble lays,
To the chorus of the sky;
And in songs of grateful praise,
Glory give to God on high.

Miss Harriet Auber. (1773—1862.) 1829

1. Hark, hark, the notes of joy Roll o'er the heavenly plains, And Seraphs find em - ploy For
their sublim - est strains; Some new delight in heaven is known; Loud ring the harps a - round the throne.

56 *"Bear the Tidings round."*

2 Hark, hark, the sounds draw nigh,
The joyful hosts descend ;
Jesus forsakes the sky,
To earth His footsteps bend ;
He comes to bless our fallen race,
He comes with messages of grace.

3 Bear, bear the tidings round ;
Let every mortal know
What love in God is found,
What pity He can show :
Ye winds that blow, ye waves that roll,
Bear the glad news from pole to pole.

4 Strike, strike the harps again,
To great Immanuel's name ;
Arise, ye sons of men,
And all His grace proclaim :
Angels and men, wake every string,
'Tis God the Saviour's praise we sing.

Rev. Andrew Reed. (1787—1862.) 1842.

57 *"The Debt we owe."*

1 Come, every pious heart
That loves the Saviour's name,
Your noblest power exert
To celebrate His fame :
Tell all above, | The debt of love
And all below, | To Him you owe.

2 He left His starry crown,
And laid His robes aside ;
On wings of love came down,
And wept, and bled, and died :
What He endured, | To save our souls
O who can tell, | From death and hell.

3 From the dark grave He rose,
The mansion of the dead ;
And thence His mighty foes
In glorious triumph led :
Up through the sky | And reigns on high,
The conqueror rode, | The Saviour, God.

4 From thence He'll quickly come,
His chariot will not stay,
And bear our spirits home
To realms of endless day :
There shall we see | And ever be
His lovely face, | In His embrace,

5 Jesus, we ne'er can pay
The debt we owe Thy love ;
Yet tell us how we may
Our gratitude approve :
Our hearts, our all, | The gift though small
To Thee we give ; | Do Thou receive.

Rev. Samuel Stennett. (1727—1795.) 1787

FOLSOM. 11, 10. 25 Johann C. W. A. Mozart. (1756—1791.)

1. BRIGHTEST and best of the sons of the morn - ing, Dawn on our
dark - ness, and lend us thine aid; Star of the East, the ho -
ri - zon a - dorn - ing, Guide where our in - fant Re - deem - er is laid.

58

"Star of the East."

2 Cold on His cradle the dew-drops are shining,
  Low lies His head with the beasts of the stall;
Angels adore Him in slumber reclining,
  Maker and Monarch, and Saviour of all.

3 Say, shall we yield Him in costly devotion,
  Odors of Edom, and offerings divine,
Gems of the mountain, and pearls of the ocean,
  Myrrh from the forest, or gold from the mine?

4 Vainly we offer each ample oblation;
  Vainly with gifts would His favor secure:
Richer by far is the heart's adoration;
  Dearer to God are the prayers of the poor.

5 Brightest and best of the sons of the morning,
  Dawn on our darkness, and lend us Thine aid;
Star of the East, the horizon adorning,
  Guide where our infant Redeemer is laid.

Bp. Reginald Heber. (1783—1826.) 1811.

WIMBORNE. L. M. John Whitaker. 1839.

1. ALL praise to Thee, e - ter - nal Lord, Clothed in the garb of flesh and blood;
Choosing a man - ger for Thy throne, While worlds on worlds are Thine a - lone.

59 *"Gelobet seist Du, Jesu Christ."*

2 Once did the skies before Thee bow;
A virgin's arms contain Thee now:
Angels who did in Thee rejoice
Now listen for Thine infant voice.

3 A little child, Thou art our guest,
That weary ones in Thee may rest;
Forlorn and lowly in Thy birth,
That we may rise to heaven from earth.

4 All this for us Thy love hath done;
By this to Thee our love is won:
For this we tune our cheerful lays,
And shout our thanks in ceaseless praise.

Martin Luther. (1483—1546.) 1524. ab.

60 *"Hosanna in the highest."*

1 WHAT are those soul-reviving strains
Which echo thus from Salem's plains?
What anthems loud, and louder still,
Sweetly resound from Zion's hill?

2 Lo, 'tis an infant chorus sings
Hosanna to the King of kings.
The Saviour comes, and babes proclaim
Salvation sent in Jesus' name.

3 Nor these alone their voice shall raise,
For we will join this song of praise:
Still Israel's children forward press,
To hail the Lord their Righteousness

4 Messiah's name shall joy impart
Alike to Jew and Gentile heart;
He bled for us, He bled for you,
And we will sing hosanna too.

5 Proclaim hosannas, loud and clear;
See David's Son and Lord appear
Glory and praise on earth be given;
Hosanna in the highest heaven.

James Montgomery. (1771—1854.) 1824.

HAMBURG (GREGORIAN.) L. M. 27 Arr. by Lowell Mason. (1792—1872.) 1825.

1. My dear Re-deem-er, and my Lord, I read my du - ty in Thy word;
But in Thy life the law ap - pears, Drawn out in liv - ing char - ac - ters.

61

The Example of Christ.

1 Pet. ii. 21.

2 Such was Thy truth, and such Thy zeal,
Such deference to Thy Father's will,
Such love and meekness so divine,
I would transcribe and make them mine.

3 Cold mountains and the midnight air
Witnessed the fervor of Thy prayer;
The desert Thy temptations knew,
Thy conflict and Thy victory too.

4 Be Thou my pattern; make me bear
More of Thy gracious image here;
Then God, the Judge, shall own my name
Amongst the followers of the Lamb.

Rev. Isaac Watts. (1674—1748.) 1709.

62

"Just as I am."

John vi. 37.

1 JUST as I am, without one plea,
But that Thy blood was shed for me,
And that Thou bidd'st me come to Thee;
O Lamb of God, I come, I come.

2 Just as I am, and waiting not
To rid my soul of one dark blot,
To Thee, whose blood can cleanse each spot,
O Lamb of God, I come.

3 Just as I am, though tossed about
With many a conflict, many a doubt,
With fears within, and foes without,
O Lamb of God, I come.

4 Just as I am, poor, wretched, blind,
Sight, riches, healing of the mind,
Yea, all I need, in Thee to find,
O Lamb of God, I come.

5 Just as I am, Thou wilt receive,
Wilt welcome, pardon, cleanse, relieve:
Because Thy promise I believe,
O Lamb of God, I come.

6 Just as I am, Thy love unknown
Has broken every barrier down:
Now, to be Thine, yea *Thine alone*,
O Lamb of God, I come.

Miss Charlotte Elliott. (1789—1871.) 1836.

AVON. C. M. — Hugh Wilson 1768.

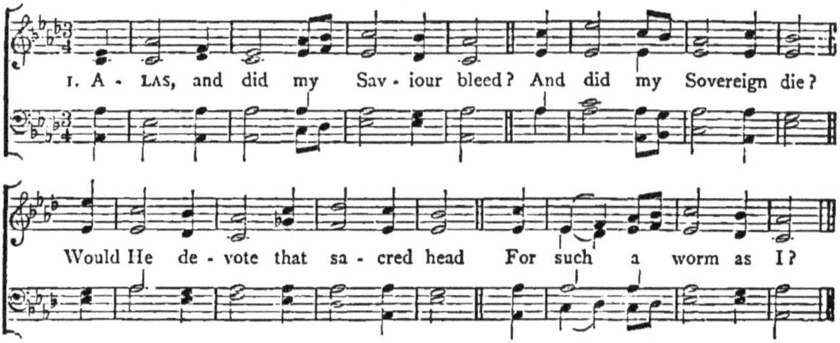
1. A - LAS, and did my Sav - iour bleed? And did my Sovereign die?
Would He de - vote that sa - cred head For such a worm as I?

63

Godly Sorrow in View of Christ's Sufferings.

2 Was it for crimes that I had done
He groaned upon the tree?
Amazing pity! grace unknown,
And love beyond degree!

3 Well might I hide my blushing face,
While His dear cross appears,
Dissolve my heart in thankfulness,
And melt mine eyes to tears.

4 But drops of grief can ne'er repay
The debt of love I owe:
Here, Lord, I give myself away;
'Tis all that I can do.

Rev. Isaac Watts. (1674—1748.) 1709. ab.

64

Kneeling at the Cross.

1 O JESUS, sweet the tears I shed,
While at Thy cross I kneel,
Gaze on Thy wounded, fainting head,
And all Thy sorrows feel.

2 My heart dissolves to see Thee bleed,
This heart so hard before;
I hear Thee for the guilty plead,
And grief o'erflows the more.

3 'Twas for the sinful Thou didst die,
And I a sinner stand:
What love speaks from Thy dying eye,
And from each piercèd hand.

4 I know this cleansing blood of Thine
Was shed, dear Lord, for me:
For me, for all, O grace divine!
Who look by faith on Thee.

5 O Christ of God, O spotless Lamb,
By love my soul is drawn;
Henceforth, forever, Thine I am;
Here life and peace are born.

6 In patient hope, the cross I'll bear,
Thine arm shall be my stay;
And Thou, enthroned, my soul shalt spare,
On Thy great judgment-day.

Rev. Ray Palmer. (1808—). 1867.

65 *Returning to God.*

1 O THOU, whose tender mercy hears
Contrition's humble sigh,
Whose hand indulgent wipes the tears
From sorrow's weeping eye;

2 See, low before Thy throne of grace,
A wretched wanderer mourn;
Hast Thou not bid me seek Thy face?
Hast Thou not said, return?

3 And shall my guilty fears prevail
To drive me from Thy feet?
O let not this dear refuge fail,
This only safe retreat!

4 O shine on this benighted heart,
With beams of mercy shine!
And let Thy healing voice impart
A taste of joys divine.

5 Thy presence only can bestow
Delights which never cloy:
Be this my solace here below,
And my eternal joy!

Miss Anne Steele. (1717—1778.) 1760. ab.

66 "*Remember me.*"

1 JESUS, Thou art the sinner's Friend·
As such I look to Thee;
Now, in the fullness of Thy love,
O Lord, remember me.

2 Remember Thy pure word of grace,
Remember Calvary;
Remember all Thy dying groans,
And then remember me.

3 Thou wondrous Advocate with God,
I yield myself to Thee;
While Thou art sitting on Thy throne,
Dear Lord, remember me.

4 Lord, I am guilty, I am vile,
But Thy salvation's free;
Then in Thine all-abounding grace,
Dear Lord, remember me.

5 And when I close my eyes in death,
When creature-helps all flee,
Then, O my dear Redeemer God,
I pray, remember me.

Rev. Richard Burnham. (1749—1810.) 1783. ab.

67 *Coming to Christ.*

1 APPROACH, my soul, the mercy-seat,
Where Jesus answers prayer;
There humbly fall before His feet,
For none can perish there.

2 Thy promise is my only plea,
With this I venture nigh;
Thou callest burdened souls to Thee,
And such, O Lord, am I.

3 Bowed down beneath a load of sin,
By Satan sorely prest,
By war without, and fears within,
I come to Thee for rest.

4 Be Thou my shield and hiding-place,
That, sheltered near Thy side,
I may my fierce accuser face,
And tell him, Thou hast died.

5 O wondrous love to bleed and die,
To bear the cross and shame,
That guilty sinners, such as I,
Might plead Thy gracious Name.

Rev. John Newton. (1725—1807.) 1779. ab.

68 "*Unto thee, and to thy Seed after thee.*" Gen. xvii. 7.

1 How large the promise, how divine,
To Abraham and his seed;
"I'll be a God to thee and thine,
Supplying all their need."

2 Jesus the ancient faith confirms,
To our great fathers given;
He takes young children to His arms,
And calls them heirs of heaven.

3 Our God, how faithful are His ways!
His love endures the same;
Nor from the promise of His grace
Blots out the children's name.

Rev. Isaac Watts. 1709. ab.

PASSION CHORALE. 7, 6. D.

Hans Leo Hassler. (1564—16 1601.
Har. by Johann Sebastian Bach. (1685—1750.)

1. { O sa - cred Head, now wound - ed, With grief and shame weighed down,
Now scorn - ful - ly sur - round - ed With thorns, Thine on - ly crown; }
O sa - cred Head, what glo - ry, What bliss, till now was Thine!
Yet, though des - pised and go - ry, I joy to call Thee mine.

69 *"Salve, caput cruentatum."*

2 What Thou, my Lord, hast suffered
Was all for sinners' gain:
Mine, mine was the transgression,
But Thine the deadly pain:
Lo, here I fall, my Saviour!
'Tis I deserve Thy place;
Look on me with Thy favor,
Vouchsafe to me Thy grace.

3 What language shall I borrow
To thank Thee, dearest Friend,
For this Thy dying sorrow,
Thy pity without end?
O make me Thine forever;
And should I fainting be,
Lord, let me never, never,
Outlive my love to Thee.

4 Be near me when I'm dying,
O show Thy cross to me;
And for my succor flying,
Come, Lord, and set me free:
These eyes, new faith receiving,
From Jesus shall not move;
For he who dies believing,
Dies safely, through Thy love.

Bernard of Clairvaux. (1091—1153.)
Rev. Paul Gerhardt. (1606—1670.) 1659.
Rev. James Waddell Alexander. (1804—1859.) 1849. ab.

FEDERAL STREET. L. M.

Henry Kemble Oliver. (1800—) 1832.

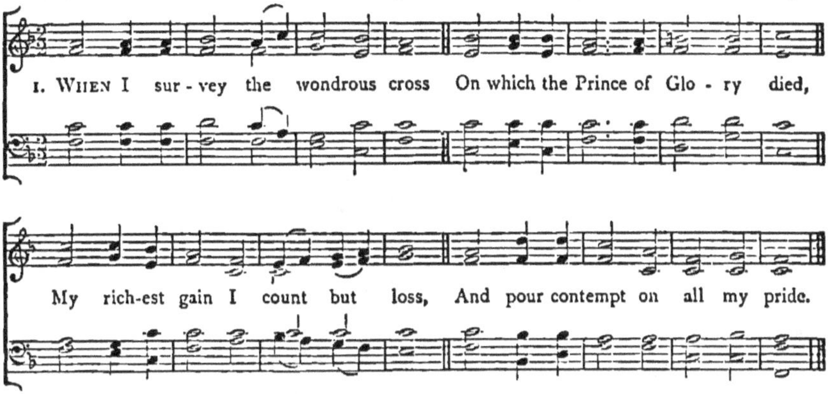
1. WHEN I sur - vey the wondrous cross On which the Prince of Glo - ry died,
My rich-est gain I count but loss, And pour contempt on all my pride.

70 *Crucifixion to the World.*

2 Forbid it, Lord, that I should boast,
Save in the death of Christ, my God:
All the vain things that charm me most,
I sacrifice them to His blood.

3 See, from His head, His hands, His feet,
Sorrow and love flow mingled down:
Did e'er such love and sorrow meet,
Or thorns compose so rich a crown?

4 His dying crimson, like a robe,
Spreads o'er His body on the tree;
Then am I dead to all the globe,
And all the globe is dead to me.

5 Were the whole realm of nature mine,
That were a present far too small:
Love so amazing, so divine,
Demands my soul, my life, my all.

Rev. Isaac Watts. (1674—1748.) 1709.

71 *"It is finished!"*

John xix. 30.

1 "'TIS finished!" so the Saviour cried,
And meekly bowed His head, and died:
"'Tis finished!" yes, the race is run,
The battle fought, the victory won.

2 'Tis finished! all that heaven decreed,
And all the ancient Prophets said
Is now fulfilled, as was designed,
In Me, the Saviour of mankind.

3 'Tis finished! this My dying groan
Shall sins of every kind atone;
Millions shall be redeemed from death,
By this My last expiring breath.

4 'Tis finished! let the joyful sound
Be heard through all the nations round;
'Tis finished! let the echo fly
Thro' heaven and hell, thro' earth and sky

Rev. Samuel Stennett. (1727—1795.) 1778. ab.

MARTYN. 7. D. **32** Simeon Butler Marsh. (1798—) 1834.

1. MA - RY to her Saviour's tomb Hast - ed at the ear - ly dawn;
Spice she brought and sweet per - fume; But the Lord she loved was gone.
For a - while she weep - ing stood, Struck with sor - row and sur - prise,
Shed - ding tears, a plenteous flood, For her heart sup - plied her eyes.

72

Weeping Mary.
John xx. 11—16.

2 Jesus, who is always near,
  Though too often unperceived,
Came, His drooping child to cheer,
  Kindly asking why she grieved.
Though at first she knew Him not,
  When He called her by her name,
Then her griefs were all forgot,
  For she found He was the same.

3 Grief and sighing quickly fled
  When she heard His welcome voice;
Just before, she thought Him dead,
  Now, He bids her heart rejoice.
What a change His word can make,
  Turning darkness into day!
You who weep for Jesus' sake,
  He will wipe your tears away.

4 He who came to comfort her,
  When she thought her all was lost,
Will for your relief appear,
  Though you now are tempest-tost.
On His word your burden cast,
  On His love your thoughts employ;
Weeping for a while may last,
  But the morning brings the joy.

Rev. John Newton. (1725—1807.) 1779

1 "CHRIST, the Lord, is risen to - day," Sons of men and an-gels say.
Raise your joys and tri-umphs high; Sing, ye heavens; and earth, re - ply.

73

"He is risen."
Mark xvi. 6.

1 "CHRIST, the Lord, is risen to-day,"
Sons of men and angels say.
Raise your joys and triumphs high;
Sing, ye heavens; and earth, reply.

2 Love's redeeming work is done,
Fought the fight, the battle won.
Lo, our Sun's eclipse is o'er;
Lo, He sets in blood no more.

3 Lives again our glorious King:
Where, O Death, is now thy sting?
Once He died our souls to save:
Where thy victory, O grave?

4 Soar we now where Christ has led,
Following our exalted Head:
Made like Him, like Him we rise;
Ours the Cross, the grave, the skies.

Rev. Charles Wesley. (1708—1788.) 1739. ab. and alt.

74

"The Lord is risen."

1 CHRIST, the Lord, is risen to-day,
Our triumphant holy-day:
He endured the Cross and grave,
Sinners to redeem and save.

2 Lo, He rises, mighty King:
Where, O death, is now thy sting?
Lo, He claims His native sky:
Grave, where is thy victory?

3 Sinners, see your ransom paid,
Peace with God forever made:
With your risen Saviour rise;
Claim with Him the purchased skies.

4 Christ, the Lord, is risen to-day,
Our triumphant holy-day;
Loud the song of victory raise;
Shout the great Redeemer's praise.

Rev. Josiah Pratt's (1768—1844.) Collection. 1829.

75

The Women at the Sepulchre.
Luke xxiv. 1—10.

1 HAIL to Thee, our risen King,
Joyfully Thy praise we sing;
For, the mighty conflict o'er,
Now Thou livest evermore.

2 Thou within the tomb hast slept,
Angel-guards Thy vigil kept:
'Twas their word to Mary brought
Tidings of the Lord she sought:—

3 "Seek Him not among the dead,
He is risen, as He said;"
Gladdened by the angelic word,
Turning, she beheld her Lord.

4 Fain like Mary, Lord, would we
In Thy glorious presence be;
Hear Thy voice, behold Thy face,
Praise Thee for Thy wondrous grace.

S. A. 1862. ab.

1. OUR Lord is ris - en from the dead, Our Je - sus is gone up on high;
The powers of hell are captive led, Dragged to the por - tals of the sky.

76

"Our Lord is risen."

Ps. xxiv.

2 There His triumphal chariot waits,
And angels chant the solemn lay:—
"Lift up your heads, ye heavenly gates,
Ye everlasting doors, give way.

3 "Loose all your bars of massy light,
And wide unfold the ethereal scene;
He claims these mansions as His right;
Receive the King of glory in."

4 "Who is this King of glory, who?"
"The Lord of glorious power possessed,
The King of saints and angels, too:
God over all, forever blest."

Rev Charles Wesley. (1708—1788.) 1743. ab.

77

"He lives."

1 "I KNOW that my Redeemer lives:"
What comfort this sweet sentence gives,
He lives, He lives, who once was dead,
He lives, my ever-living H ad.

2 He lives to bless me with His love,
He lives to plead for me above,
He lives my hungry soul to feed,
He lives to help in time of need.

3 He lives to silence all my fears,
He lives to stoop and wipe my tears,
He lives to calm my troubled heart,
He lives all blessings to impart.

4 He lives, all glory to His Name;
He lives, my Jesus, still the same:
O the sweet joy this sentence gives,
"I know that my Redeemer lives."

Rev. Samuel Medley. (1738—1799.) 1789. ab. and sl. alt.

78

Prayer for Speedy Triumph.

1 SOON may the last glad song arise
Through all the millions of the skies,
That song of triumph, which records
That all the earth is now the Lord's.

2 Let thrones, and powers, and kingdoms be
Obedient, mighty God, to Thee;
And over land, and stream, and main,
Wave Thou the sceptre of Thy reign.

3 O that the anthem now might swell,
And host to host the triumph tell,
That not one rebel heart remains,
But over all the Saviour reigns.

Mrs. Voke. 1816.

VICTORY. 8, 7, 4. Harry Hobert Beadle. (1821—) 1854.

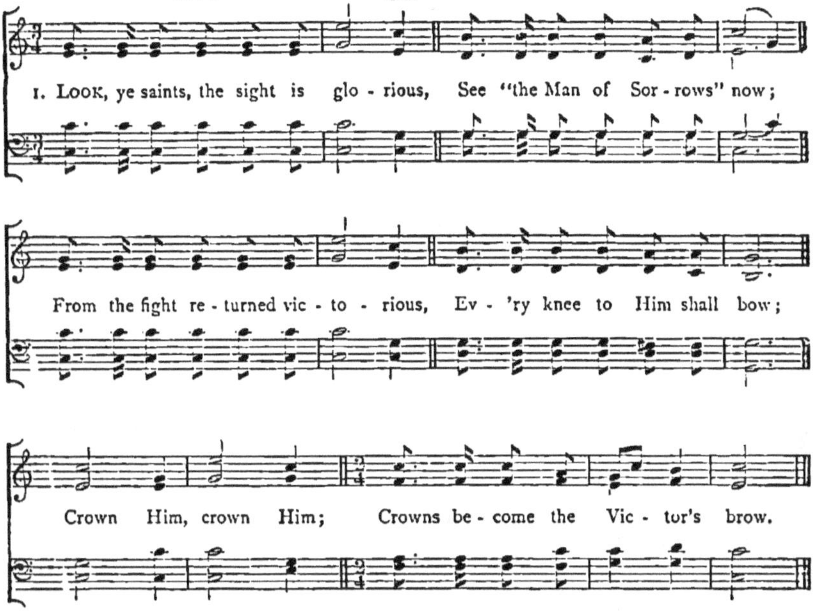
1. LOOK, ye saints, the sight is glo - rious, See "the Man of Sor - rows" now;
From the fight re - turned vic - to - rious, Ev - 'ry knee to Him shall bow;
Crown Him, crown Him; Crowns be - come the Vic - tor's brow.

79 "*And He shall reign forever and ever.*"
Rev. xi. 15.

2 Sinners in derision crowned Him,
Mocking thus the Saviour's claim;
Saints and angels crowd around Him,
Own His title, praise His name;
Crown Him, crown Him;
Spread abroad the Victor's fame.

3 Hark, those bursts of acclamation!
Hark, those loud triumphant chords!
Jesus takes the highest station:
O what joy the sight affords!
Crown Him, crown Him;
"King of kings, and Lord of lords."

Rev. Thomas Kelly. (1769—1855.) 1809.

80 "*Thou art worthy, O Lord.*"
Rev. iv. 11.

1 GLORY, glory everlasting
Be to Him who bore the cross!
Who redeemed our souls, by tasting
Death, the death deserved by us;
Spread His glory,
Who redeemed His people thus.

2 His is love, 'tis love unbounded,
Without measure, without end;
Human thought is here confounded,
'Tis too vast to comprehend
Praise the Saviour!
Magnify the sinner's Friend.

3 While we hear the wondrous story
Of the Saviour's cross and shame,
Sing we "Everlasting glory
Be to God, and to the Lamb:"
Saints and angels,
Give ye glory to His name.

Rev. Thomas Kelly. 1809.

BROWN. C. M. 36 William Batchelder Bradbury. (1816—1868.) 1844.

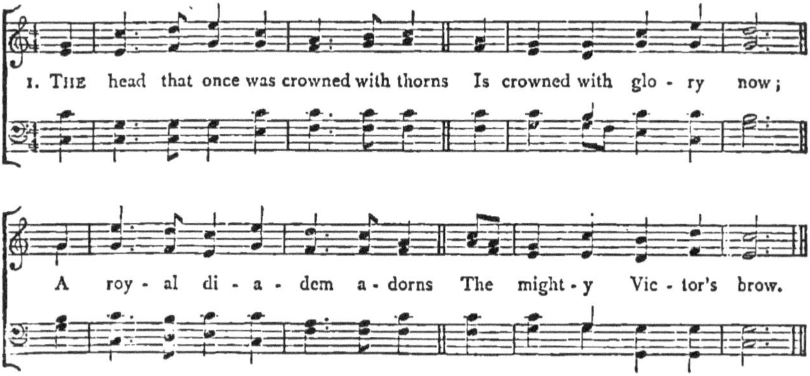
1. THE head that once was crowned with thorns Is crowned with glo - ry now;
A roy - al di - a - dem a - dorns The might - y Vic - tor's brow.

81 *"Perfect through Sufferings."*
Heb. ii. 10.

2 The highest place that heaven affords
Is His, is His by right,
"The King of kings, and Lord of lords,"
And heaven's eternal light.

3 The joy of all who dwell above,
The joy of all below
To whom He manifests His love,
And grants His name to know:

4 To them the cross, with all its shame,
With all its grace, is given;
Their name, an everlasting name,
Their joy, the joy of heaven.

5 The cross He bore is life and health,
Though shame and death to Him;
His people's hope, His people's wealth,
Their everlasting theme.

Rev. Thomas Kelly. (1769—1855.) 1820.

82 *"The Desire of all Nations."*
Hag. ii. 7.

1 INFINITE excellence is Thine,
Thou glorious Prince of Grace!
Thy uncreated beauties shine
With never-fading rays.

2 Sinners, from earth's remotest end,
Come bending at Thy feet;
To Thee their prayers and songs ascend,
In Thee their wishes meet.

3 Millions of happy spirits live
On Thy exhaustless store;
From Thee they all their bliss receive,
And still Thou givest more.

4 Thou art their triumph, and their joy;
They find their all in Thee;
Thy glories will their tongues employ
Through all eternity.

Rev. John Fawcett. (1739—1817.) 1782. ab.

83 *"The Way, the Truth, the Life."*
John xiv. 6.

1 THOU art the Way: to Thee alone
From sin and death we flee;
And he who would the Father seek,
Must seek Him, Lord, by Thee.

2 Thou art the Truth: Thy word alone
True wisdom can impart;
Thou only canst inform the mind
And purify the heart.

3 Thou art the Life: the rending tomb
Proclaims Thy conquering arm,
And those who put their trust in Thee
Nor death, nor hell shall harm.

4 Thou art the Way, the Truth, the Life;
Grant us that Way to know,
That Truth to keep, that Life to win,
Whose joys eternal flow.
Bp. George Washington Doane. (1799—1859). 1824.

84

A Lamp, and a Light.
Ps. cxix. 105. 2 Tim. iii. 16.

1 HOW precious is the book divine,
By inspiration given:
Bright as a lamp its doctrines shine,
To guide our souls to heaven.

2 Its light, descending from above,
Our gloomy world to cheer,
Displays a Saviour's boundless love,
And brings His glories near.

3 It shows to man his wandering ways,
And where his feet have trod;
And brings to view the matchless grace
Of a forgiving God.

4 It sweetly cheers our drooping hearts,
In this dark vale of tears;
Life, light, and joy it still imparts,
And quells our rising fears.

5 This lamp, through all the tedious night
Of life, shall guide our way,
Till we behold the clearer light
Of an eternal day.
Rev. John Fawcett. (1739—1817.) 1782. ab.

85

Jacob's Vow.
Gen. xxviii. 20—22.

1 O GOD of Bethel, by whose hand
Thy people still are fed;
Who through this weary pilgrimage
Hast all our fathers led:

2 Our vows, our prayers, we now present
Before Thy throne of grace:
God of our fathers, be the God
Of their succeeding race.

3 Through each perplexing path of life
Our wandering footsteps guide;
Give us each day our daily bread,
And raiment fit provide.

4 O spread Thy covering wings around,
Till all our wanderings cease,
And, at our Father's loved abode,
Our souls arrive in peace.

5 Such blessings from Thy gracious hand
Our humble prayers implore;
And Thou shalt be our chosen God
And portion evermore.
Rev. Philip Doddridge. (1702—1751.) 1737.
Michael Bruce. (1746—1767). 1781. alt.

86

The Shepherd of Israel.
Ps. lxxx. 1.

1 SHEPHERD of Israel, from above
Thy feeble flock behold;
And never let us lose Thy love,
Nor wander from Thy fold.

2 Thou wilt not cast Thy lambs away;
Thy hand is ever near,
To guide them lest they go astray,
And keep them safe from fear.

3 Thy tender care supports the weak,
And will not let them fall;
Then teach us, Lord, Thy praise to speak
And on Thy name to call.

4 We want Thy help, for we are frail;
Thy light, for we are blind;
Let grace o'er all our doubts prevail,
To prove that Thou art kind.

5 Guide us through life; and when at last
We enter into rest,
Thy tender arms around us cast,
And fold us to Thy breast.
Rev. William Hiley Bathurst. (1796—) 1831. ab.

HARWELL. 8, 7. 61 Lowell Mason. (1792—1872.) 1840.

1. { HARK, ten thousand harps and voices Sound the note of praise a - bove! } See, He sits
{ Jesus reigns, and heaven re-joices; Je - sus reigns, the God of love; } See, He sits on yonder throne;
Je - sus rules
Je - sus rules the world a - lone, See, He sits on yonder throne; Je-sus rules the world a - lone.

87

Worshipped of Angels.

Heb. i. 6.

2 King of glory, reign forever!
Thine an everlasting crown;
Nothing from Thy love shall sever
Those whom Thou hast made Thine own;
Happy objects of Thy grace,
Destined to behold Thy face.

3 Saviour, hasten Thine appearing;
Bring, O bring the glorious day,
When the awful summons hearing,
Heaven and earth shall pass away:
Then, with golden harps, we'll sing,
"Glory, glory to our King!"

Rev. Thomas Kelly. 1847. ab.

88

A Hymn of Praise to the Redeemer.

1 COME, ye faithful, raise the anthem,
Cleave the skies with shouts of praise;
Sing to Him who found the ransom,
Ancient of eternal days:
God Eternal, Word Incarnate,
Whom the Heaven of heaven obeys.

2 Ere He raised the lofty mountains,
Formed the sea, or built the sky,
Love eternal, free, and boundless,
Forced the Lord of life to die:
Lifted up the Prince of princes
On the throne of Calvary.

3 Now on those eternal mountains
Stands the sapphire throne, all bright,
Where unceasing hallelujahs
They upraise, the sons of light:
Zion's people tell His praises,
Victor after hard-won fight.

4 Bring your harps and bring your incense,
Sweep the string and pour the lay;
Let the earth proclaim His wonders,
King of that celestial day:
He, the Lamb once slain, is worthy,
Who was dead and lives for aye.

Rev. Job Hupton. (1762—1849) 1808. ab.
Alt. by Rev. John Mason Neale. (1818—1866.) 1852.

CORONATION. C. M. Oliver Holden. (1756—1831.) 1793.

1. All hail the power of Je - sus' name! Let an - gels pros - trate fall,
Bring forth the roy - al di - a - dem, And crown Him Lord of all,
Bring forth the roy - al di - a - dem, And crown Him Lord of all.

89 *"Lord of all."*
Acts x. 36.

2 Crown Him, ye morning stars of light,
Who fixed this floating ball;
Now hail the strength of Israel's might,
And crown Him Lord of all.

3 Sinners, whose love can ne'er forget
The wormwood and the gall,
Go, spread your trophies at His feet,
And crown Him Lord of all.

4 Let every kindred, every tribe,
On this terrestrial ball,
To Him all majesty ascribe,
And crown Him Lord of all.

Rev. Edward Perronet. (—1792.) 1780. ab. and alt

90 *The Lamb worshipped by all Creatures.*
Rev. v. 11—13.

1 Come, let us join our cheerful songs
With angels round the throne;
Ten thousand thousand are their tongues,
But all their joys are one.

2 "Worthy the Lamb that died," they cry,
"To be exalted thus;"
"Worthy the Lamb," our lips reply,
"For He was slain for us."

3 Jesus is worthy to receive
Honor and power divine;
And blessings more than we can give,
Be, Lord, forever Thine.

4 Let all that dwell above the sky,
And air, and earth, and seas,
Conspire to lift Thy glories high,
And speak Thine endless praise.

Rev. Isaac Watts. 1709

91 *"Hosanna to our conquering King."*

1 Hosanna to our conquering King,
All hail, incarnate Love!
Ten thousand songs and glories wait
To crown Thy head above.

2 Thy victories, and Thy deathless fame,
Through the wide world shall run,
And everlasting ages sing
The triumphs Thou hast won.

Rev. Isaac Watts. 1790. ab.

AUTUMN. 8, 7. D. Spanish Melody. From Marechio.

1. HAIL, Thou once de - spis - éd Je - sus, Hail, thou Ga - li - le - an king!
Thou didst suf - fer to re - lease us, Thou didst free sal - va - tion bring:
D. S. By Thy mer - its we find fa - vor; Life is giv - en through Thy Name.
Fine.
Hail, Thou ag - o - niz - ing Sav - iour, Bear - er of our sin and shame
D. S.

92 "*Enthroned in Glory.*"

2 Paschal Lamb, by God appointed,
  All our sins on Thee were laid:
By Almighty love anointed,
  Thou hast full atonement made;
All Thy people are forgiven
  Through the virtue of Thy blood;
Opened is the gate of heaven;
  Peace is made 'twixt man and God.

3 Jesus, hail, enthroned in glory,
  There forever to abide;
All the heavenly hosts adore Thee,
  Seated at Thy Father's side.
There for sinners Thou art pleading;
  There Thou dost our place prepare;
Ever for us interceding
  Till in glory we appear.

Rev. John Bakewell. (1721—1819.) 1760. alt.
Rev. Augustus Montague Toplady. (1740—1778.) 1776.

93 "*Thou art worthy.*"

(Second Part of preceding Hymn.)

1 WORSHIP, honor, power, and blessing,
  Thou art worthy to receive;
Loudest praises without ceasing,
  Meet it is for us to give.
Help, ye bright angelic spirits,
  Bring your sweetest, noblest lays;
Help to sing our Saviour's merits,
  Help to chant Immanuel's praise.

2 Soon we shall, with those in glory,
  His transcendent grace relate;
Gladly sing the amazing story
  Of His dying love so great;
In that blessed contemplation
  We for evermore shall dwell,
Crowned with bliss and consolation,
  Such as none below can tell.

Rev. John Bakewell. 1760 alt.
Rev. Augustus Montague Toplady. 1776.

94 "*Love Divine.*"

1 Love Divine, all love excelling,
Joy of heaven, to earth come down;
Fix in us Thy humble dwelling,
All Thy faithful mercies crown:
Jesus, Thou art all compassion,
Pure, unbounded love Thou art:
Visit us with Thy salvation,
Enter every trembling heart.

2 Breathe, O breathe, Thy loving Spirit
Into every troubled breast;
Let us all in Thee inherit,
Let us find that second rest;
Take away our power of sinning,
Alpha and Omega be;
End of faith, as its beginning,
Set our hearts at liberty.

3 Come, almighty to deliver,
Let us all Thy life receive;
Suddenly return, and never,
Never more Thy temples leave.
Thee we would be always blessing,
Serve Thee as Thy hosts above,
Pray and praise Thee without ceasing,
Glory in Thy perfect love.

Rev. Charles Wesley. (1708–1788.) 1747. ab. and sl. alt.

95 *Sowing and Reaping.*

1 He that goeth forth with weeping,
Bearing precious seed in love,
Never tiring, never sleeping,
Findeth mercy from above;
Soft descend the dews of heaven,
Bright the rays celestial shine;
Precious fruits will thus be given,
Through an influence all divine.

2 Sow thy seed, be never weary,
Let no fears thy soul annoy;
Be the prospect ne'er so dreary,
Thou shalt reap the fruits of joy.
Lo, the scene of verdure brightening,
See the rising grain appear;
Look again: the fields are whitening,
For the harvest time is near.

Thomas Hastings. (1784–1872.) 1836.

96 *The City of God.*
Is. xxxiii. 20, 21.

1 Glorious things of thee are spoken,
Zion, city of our God;
He whose word cannot be broken,
Formed thee for His own abode:
On the Rock of Ages founded,
What can shake thy sure repose?
With salvation's walls surrounded,
Thou mayest smile at all thy foes.

2 See, the streams of living waters,
Springing from eternal love,
Well supply thy sons and daughters,
And all fear of want remove:
Who can faint, while such a river
Ever flows their thirst t' assuage?
Grace, which, like the Lord, the Giver,
Never fails from age to age.

3 Round each habitation hovering,
See the cloud and fire appear,
For a glory and a covering,
Showing that the Lord is near:
Thus deriving from their banner
Light by night, and shade by day,
Safe they feed upon the manna
Which He gives them when they pray

Rev. John Newton. (1725–1807.) 1779.

97 "*Come over and help us.*"
Acts xvi. 9.

1 Hark, what mean those lamentations,
Rolling sadly through the sky?
'Tis the cry of heathen nations,
"Come and help us, or we die."
Lost and helpless and desponding,
Wrapt in error's night they lie;
To their cries your hearts responding,
Haste to help them ere they die.

2 Hark, again those lamentations
Rolling sadly through the sky;
Louder cry the heathen nations,
"Come and help us, or we die."
Hear the heathens' sad complaining;
Christians, hear their dying cry;
And the love of Christ constraining,
Join to help them ere they die.

Rev. John Cawood. (1775–1852.) 1819. alt.

OAKSVILLE. C. M. Charles Zeuner. (1795—1857.) 1839

1. No track is on the sun - ny sky, No foot - prints on the air;
Je - sus hath gone; the face of earth Is des - o - late and bare.

98 *Pentecost.*
Acts ii. 1—4.

2 That Upper Room is heaven on earth:
Within its precincts lie
All that earth has of faith, or hope,
Or heaven-born charity.

3 He comes! He comes! that mighty Breath
From heaven's eternal shores;
His uncreated freshness fills
His Bride as she adores.

4 The Spirit came into the Church
With His unfailing power;
He is the living Heart that beats
Within her at this hour.

5 Most tender Spirit, mighty God,
Sweet must Thy presence be,
If loss of Jesus can be gain,
So long as we have Thee!

Rev. Frederick William Faber. (1814—1863.) 1849.
ab. and sl. alt.

99 *The Promise fulfilled.*

1 Let songs of praises fill the sky:
Christ, our ascended Lord,
Sends down His Spirit from on high,
According to His word.

2 The Spirit by His heavenly breath,
New life creates within;
He quickens sinners from the death
Of trespasses and sin.

3 The things of Christ the Spirit takes,
And shows them unto men;
The fallen soul His temple makes
God's image stamps again.

4 Come, Holy Spirit, from above,
With Thy celestial fire;
Come, and with flames of zeal and love,
Our hearts and tongues inspire.

Rev. Thomas Cotterill. (1779—1823.) 1819. ab.

100 *"The Comforter is Come."*

1 My God, my reconciled God,
Creator of my peace:
Thee will I love, and praise, and sing,
Till life and breath shall cease.

2 My soul doth magnify the Lord,
My spirit doth rejoice
In God my Saviour and my God;
I hear His joyful voice.

3 My God, my reconciled God,
Creator of my peace:
Thee will I love, and praise, and sing,
Till life and breath shall cease.

Rev. John Mason. (—1694) 1683. ab.

DENFIELD. (AZMON.) C. M. 43

Carl Gotthilf Gläser. (1784—1829.) 1828.
Arr. by Lowell Mason. (1792—1872.) 1839.

1. COME, Ho - ly Spir - it, heavenly Dove, With all Thy quickening powers,
Kin - dle a flame of sa - cred love In these cold hearts of ours.

101 *Breathing after the Holy Spirit.*

2 In vain we tune our formal songs,
  In vain we strive to rise;
Hosannas languish on our tongues,
  And our devotion dies.

3 Dear Lord, and shall we ever live
  At this poor dying rate,
Our love so faint, so cold to Thee,
  And Thine to us so great?

4 Come, Holy Spirit, heavenly Dove,
  With all Thy quickening powers,
Come, shed abroad a Saviour's love,
  And that shall kindle ours.

Rev. Isaac Watts. 1709.

102 *For a well-grounded Hope of Salvation.*

1 ETERNAL Spirit, Source of truth,
  Our contrite hearts inspire:
Kindle the flame of heavenly love,
  And feed the pure desire.

2 'Tis Thine to soothe the sorrowing mind
  With Satan's yoke oppressed;
'Tis Thine to bid the dying live,
  And give the weary rest.

3 Subdue the power of every sin,
  Whate'er that sin may be;
That we, in singleness of heart,
  May worship only Thee.

4 Then with our spirits witness bear
  That we're the sons of God,
Redeemed from sin, and death, and hell,
  Through Christ's atoning blood.

Rev. Joseph Hart. (1712—1768.) 1759. much alt.
Rev. Thomas Cotterill. (1779—1823.) 1810. ab.

103 *"Make me a clean Heart."*
Ps. li. 10.

1 O FOR a heart to praise my God,
  A heart from sin set free;
A heart that always feels Thy blood
  So freely spilt for me!

2 A heart resigned, submissive, meek,
  My dear Redeemer's throne;
Where only Christ is heard to speak,
  Where Jesus reigns alone.

3 A humble, lowly, contrite heart,
  Believing, true, and clean;
Which neither life nor death can part
  From Him that dwells within.

4 Thy nature, dearest Lord, impart;
  Come quickly from above;
Write Thy new Name upon my heart,
  Thy new, best Name of Love.

Rev. Charles Wesley. (1708—1788.) 1742. ab.

ERNAN. L. M. Lowell Mason. (1792—1872.) 1850.

1. Come, O Cre-a - tor - Spir - it blest, And in our souls take up Thy rest;
Come, with Thy grace and heavenly aid, To fill the hearts which Thou hast made.

104 *"Veni Creator Spiritus."*

2 Great Comforter, to Thee we cry;
O highest gift of God most high,
O Fount of life, O Fire of love,
And sweet anointing from above!

3 Kindle our senses from above,
And make our hearts o'erflow with love;
With patience firm, and virtue high,
The weakness of our flesh supply.

4 Far from us drive the foe we dread,
And grant us Thy true peace instead;
So shall we not, with Thee for guide,
Turn from the path of life aside.

Unknown Author of the 7th or 8th Century.
Tr. by Rev. Edward Caswall. (1814—) 1849. ab. and alt.

105 *Teachings of the Spirit.*

1 Come, blessèd Spirit, Source of light,
Whose power and grace are unconfined
Dispel the gloomy shades of night,
The thicker darkness of the mind.

2 To mine illumined eyes display
The glorious truths Thy word reveals;
Cause me to run the heavenly way;
The book unfold, and loose the seals.

3 Thine inward teachings make me know
The mysteries of redeeming love,
The vanity of things below,
And excellence of things above.

4 While through this dubious maze I stray,
Spread, like the sun, Thy beams abroad,
To show the dangers of the way,
And guide my feeble steps to God.

Rev. Benjamin Beddome. (1717—1795.) 1818.

106 *Prayer for Rest in God.*

1 Come, Holy Spirit, calm my mind,
And fit me to approach my God;
Remove each vain, each worldly thought
And lead me to Thy blest abode.

2 Hast Thou imparted to my soul
A living spark of heavenly fire?
O kindle now the sacred flame;
Teach it to burn with pure desire.

3 A brighter faith and hope impart,
And let me now the Saviour see:
O soothe and cheer my burdened heart,
And bid my spirit rest in Thee.

Rev. Henry Forster Burder's Coll. 1826.

UXBRIDGE. L. M. Lowell Mason. (1792—1872.) 1830.

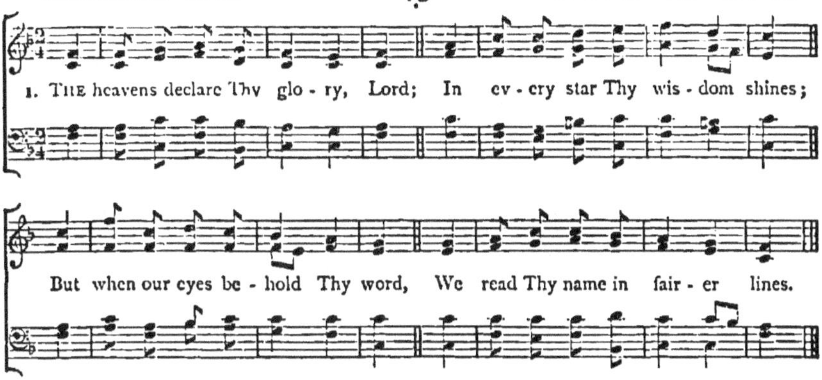
1. THE heavens declare Thy glo - ry, Lord; In ev - ery star Thy wis - dom shines;
But when our eyes be - hold Thy word, We read Thy name in fair - er lines.

107

The two Revelations.
Ps. xix.

2 The rolling sun, the changing light,
And nights and days, Thy power confess,
But the blest volume Thou hast writ,
Reveals Thy justice and Thy grace.

3 Sun, moon, and stars, convey Thy praise
Round the whole earth, and never stand:
So when Thy truth began its race,
It touched and glanced on every land.

4 Great Sun of Righteousness, arise,
Bless the dark world with heavenly light;
Thy gospel makes the simple wise,
Thy laws are pure, Thy judgments right.

Rev. Isaac Watts. (1674—1748.) 1719. ab.

108

God's Word our Guide.

1 GOD, in the gospel of His Son,
Makes His eternal counsels known:
Where love in all its glory shines,
And truth is drawn in fairest lines.

2 Here sinners, of an humble frame
May taste His grace, and learn His name;
May read, in characters of blood,
The wisdom, power, and grace of God.

3 The prisoner here may break his chains,
The weary rest from all his pains;
The captive feel his bondage cease;
The mourner find the way of peace.

4 Here faith reveals to mortal eyes
A brighter world beyond the skies;
Here shines the light which guides our way
From earth to realms of endless day.

5 O grant us grace, Almighty Lord,
To read and mark Thy holy word;
Its truth with meekness to receive,
And by its holy precepts live.

Rev. Benjamin Beddome. (1717—1795.) 1787. ab. and alt. Rev. Thomas Cotterill. (1779—1823.) 1819.

HURSLEY. L. M.

Francis Joseph Haydn. (1732—1809.) 1798.
Arr. by William Henry Monk. 1861.

1. SUN of my soul, Thou Sav - iour dear, It is not night if Thou be near:
O may no earth - born cloud a - rise To hide Thee from Thy ser - vant's eyes.

109

"Abide with us."
Luke xxiv. 29.

2 When the soft dews of kindly sleep
My wearied eyelids gently steep,
Be my last thought how sweet to rest
Forever on my Saviour's breast.

3 Abide with me from morn till eve,
For without Thee I can not live;
Abide with me when night is nigh,
For without Thee I dare not die.

4 If some poor wandering child of Thine
Have spurned, to-day, the voice divine,
Now, Lord, the gracious work begin;
Let Him no more lie down in sin.

5 Watch by the sick; enrich the poor
With blessings from Thy boundless store;
Be every mourner's sleep to-night,
Like infants' slumbers, pure and light.

6 Come near and bless us when we wake,
Ere through the world our way we take;
Till, in the ocean of Thy love,
We lose ourselves in heaven above.

Rev. John Keble. (1792—1866.) 1827. ab.

110

The Lord's Day Evening.

1 SWEET Saviour, bless us ere we go;
Thy word into our minds instill;
And make our lukewarm hearts to glow
With lowly love and fervent will.

2 The day is done, its hours have run;
And Thou hast taken count of all,
The scanty triumphs grace have won,
The broken vow, the frequent fall.

3 Grant us, dear Lord, from evil ways
True absolution and release;
And bless us, more than in past days,
With purity and inward peace.

4 Do more than pardon; give us joy,
Sweet fear, and sober liberty,
And loving hearts without alloy
That only long to be like Thee.

5 For all we love, the poor, the sad,
The sinful, unto Thee we call;
O let Thy mercy make us glad;
Thou art our Jesus, and our All.

Rev. Frederick William Faber. (1814—1863.) 1849. ab.

III

Not ashamed of Jesus.
Rom. i. 16. Heb. ii. 11.

1 JESUS, and shall it ever be,
A mortal man ashamed of Thee?
Ashamed of Thee, whom angels praise,
Whose glories shine through endless days?

2 Ashamed of Jesus, that dear Friend
On whom my hopes of heaven depend!
No, when I blush, be this my shame,
That I no more revere His name.

3 Ashamed of Jesus! yes, I may
When I've no guilt to wash away,
No tear to wipe, no good to crave,
No fear to quell, no soul to save.

4 Till then, nor is my boasting vain,
Till then I boast a Saviour slain;
And oh, may this my glory be,
That Christ is not ashamed of me.

Rev. Joseph Grigg. (—1768.) 1765. alt.
Rev. Benjamin Francis. (1734—1799.) 1787.

112

Bearing the Cross for Christ.

1 MY precious Lord, for Thy dear Name
I bear the cross, despise the shame;
Nor do I faint, while Thou art near;
I lean on Thee; how can I fear?

2 No other name but Thine is given
To cheer my soul, in earth or heaven;
No other wealth will I require;
No other friend can I desire.

3 Yea, into nothing would I fall
For Thee alone, my All in all;
To feel Thy love, my only joy,
To tell Thy love my sole employ.

Moravian Collection. 1754. ab.

113

God leading us.
Ps. cvii.

1 GIVE thanks to God; He reigns above;
Kind are His thoughts, His name is love:
His mercy ages past have known,
And ages long to come shall own.

2 Let the redeemèd of the Lord
The wonders of His grace record;
Israel, the nation whom He chose,
And rescued from their mighty foes.

3 He feeds and clothes us all the way,
He guides our footsteps lest we stray;
He guards us with a powerful hand,
And brings us to the heavenly land.

4 Oh, let the saints with joy record
The truth and goodness of the Lord
How great His works! how kind His ways
Let every tongue pronounce His praise.

Rev. Isaac Watts. 1719. ab.

114

What Christ did for me.

1 IN love, the Father's sinless child
Sojourned at Nazareth for me:
With sinners dwelt the Undefiled,
The Holy One in Galilee.

2 Jesus, whom angel hosts adore,
Became a man of griefs for me;
In love, though rich, becoming poor,
That I, through Him, enriched might be

3 Though Lord of all, above, below,
He went to Olivet for me;
He drank my cup of wrath and woe,
And bled in dark Gethsemane.

4 The ever-blessed Son of God
Went up to Calvary for me;
There paid my debt, there bore my load
In His own body on the tree.

5 Jesus, whose dwelling is the skies,
Went down into the grave for me;
There overcame my enemies,
There won the glorious victory.

6 'Tis finished all: the veil is rent,
The welcome sure, the access free;
Now then, we leave our banishment,
O Father, to return to Thee!

Rev. Horatius Bonar. (1808—) 1857. ab

1. Ho - ly Bi - ble, book di - vine, Precious treasure, thou art mine;
Mine to tell me whence I came, Mine to teach me what I am.

115 *"Holy Bible, Book divine."*

2 Mine to chide me when I rove,
Mine to show a Saviour's love;
Mine art thou to guide my feet,
Mine to judge, condemn, acquit.

3 Mine to comfort in distress,
If the Holy Spirit bless;
Mine to show by living faith
Man can triumph over death.

4 Mine to tell of joys to come,
Light and life beyond the tomb;
Holy Bible, book divine,
Precious treasure, thou art mine.

John Burton. (1773—1822.) 1805. alt.

116 *"Immer muss ich wieder lesen."*

1 EVER would I fain be reading,
In the ancient holy Book,
Of my Saviour's gentle pleading,
Truth in every word and look.

2 How when children came He blessed them,
Suffered no man to reprove;
Took them in His arms and pressed them
To His heart with words of love.

3 How He healed the sick and dying,
Heard the contrite sinner's moan,
Sought the poor, and stilled their crying,
Called them brothers and His own.

4 Still I read the ancient story,
And my joy is ever new;
How for us He left His glory,
How He still is kind and true.

5 Let me kneel, my Lord, before Thee,
Let my heart in tears o'erflow,
Melted by Thy love adore Thee,
Blest in Thee 'mid joy or woe.

Miss Luise Hensel. (1798—) 1829.
Tr. by Miss Catherine Winkworth. (1829—) 1858.
ab. and alt.

117 *"Walte, walte nah und fern."*

1 SPREAD, O spread, thou mighty word,
Spread the kingdom of the Lord,
Wheresoe'er His breath has given
Life to beings meant for heaven.

2 Tell them how the Father's will
Made the world, and keeps it still;
How He sent His Son to save
All who help and comfort crave.

3 Tell of our Redeemer's love,
Who forever doth remove,
By His holy sacrifice,
All the guilt that on us lies.

4 Tell them of the Spirit given
Now, to guide us up to heaven,
Strong and holy, just and true,
Working both to will and do.

Rev. Jonathan Frederic Bahnmaier. (1774—1841). 1822.
Tr. by Miss Catherine Winkworth. 1858. ab.

ALETTA. 7. William Batchelder Bradbury. (1816—1868.) 1858.

1. GRA - CIOUS Spir - it, Dove Di - vine, Let Thy light with - in me shine;
All my guilt - y fears re - move, Fill me full of heaven and love.

118 *Prayer for Peace and Rest.*

2 Speak Thy pardoning grace to me,
Set the burdened sinner free,
Lead me to the Lamb of God,
Wash me in His precious blood.

3 Life and peace to me impart,
Seal salvation on my heart,
Breathe Thyself into my breast,
Earnest of immortal rest.

4 Let me never from Thee stray,
Keep me in the narrow way,
Fill my soul with joy divine,
Keep me, Lord, forever Thine.

John Stocker. 1776. ab.

119 *With Light, with Power, with Joy.*

1 HOLY GHOST, with light divine,
Shine upon this heart of mine;
Chase the shades of night away,
Turn the darkness into day.

2 Holy Ghost, with power divine,
Cleanse this guilty heart of mine;
Long has sin, without control,
Held dominion o'er my soul.

3 Holy Ghost, with joy divine,
Cheer this saddened heart of mine;
Bid my many woes depart.
Heal my wounded, bleeding heart.

4 Holy Spirit, all Divine,
Dwell within this heart of mine
Cast down every idol-throne;
Reign supreme, and reign alone.

Rev. Andrew Reed. (1787—1862.) 1843. ab.

120 *"Ask what I shall give thee."* 1 Kings iii. 5.

1 COME, my soul, thy suit prepare,
Jesus loves to answer prayer;
He Himself has bid thee pray,
Therefore will not say thee nay.

2 With my burden I begin,
Lord, remove this load of sin;
Let Thy blood, for sinners spilt,
Set my conscience free from guilt.

3 Lord, I come to Thee for rest,
Take possession of my breast
There Thy blood-bought right maintain,
And without a rival reign.

4 While I am a pilgrim here,
Let Thy love my spirit cheer;
As my Guide, my Guard, my Friend,
Lead me to my journey's end.

5 Show me what I have to do,
Every hour my strength renew;
Let me live a life of faith,
Let me die Thy people's death.

Rev. John Newton. (1725—1807.) 1779. ab.

SCOTLAND. 12, 11. John Clarke. (1770—1818.) 1800.

1. The voice of free grace cries, Escape to the mountain; For Adam's lost race, Christ hath
opened a fountain; { For sin, and uncleanness, and ev - ery transgress-ion, His
{ Halle- lu - jah to the Lamb, who hath purchased our pardon, We'll
blood flows most freely, in streams of salvation, His blood flows most freely, in streams of salvation. }
praise Him again, when we pass over Jordan, We'll praise Him again, when we pass over Jordan. }

121 *"The Voice of free Grace."*

2 Ye souls that are wounded, O flee to the Saviour;
He calls you in mercy, 'tis infinite favor;
Your sins are increased as high as a mountain,
His blood can remove them, it flows from the fountain.
Hallelujah, etc.

3 With joy shall we stand, when escaped to the shore;
With harps in our hands, we will praise Him the more;
We'll range the sweet plains on the banks of the river,
And sing of salvation for ever and ever.
Hallelujah to the Lamb, who hath purchased our pardon,
We'll praise Him again, when we pass over Jordan.

Rev. Richard Burdsall. (1735—1824.) 1796. ab. and alt.

122 *"O come to the merciful Saviour."*

1 O come to the merciful Saviour that calls you,
O come to the Lord who forgives and forgets;
Though dark be the fortune on earth that befalls you,
There's a bright home above, where the sun never sets.

2 O come then to Jesus, whose arms are extended
To fold His dear children in closest embrace.
O come, for your exile will shortly be ended,
And Jesus will show you His beautiful face.

3 Then come to the Saviour, whose mercy grows brighter
The longer you look at the depths of His love;
And fear not, 'tis Jesus, and life's cares grow lighter
As you think of the home and the glory above.

Rev. Frederick William Faber. (1814—1863.) 1849. ab.

 Rev. Josiah Hopkins. (1786—1862.) 1830.

1. O TURN ye, O turn ye, for why will ye die, When God in great mercy is coming so nigh?
Now Jesus invites you, the Spirit says, "come!" And angels are waiting to welcome you home

123 *"O turn ye, O turn ye."*

2 How vain the delusion, that while you delay,
Your hearts may grow better by staying [away!
Come wretched, come starving, come just as you be,
While streams of salvation are flowing so [free.

3 And now Christ is ready your souls to receive;
O how can you question, if you will believe?
If sin is your burden, why will you not come?
'Tis you He bids welcome; He bids you come home.

4 In riches, in pleasures, what can you obtain,
To soothe your affliction or banish your [pain?
To bear up your spirit when summoned to die,
Or waft you to mansions of glory on high?

5 Why will you be starving, and feeding on air?
There's mercy in Jesus, enough and to spare;
If still you are doubting, make trial and see,
And prove that His mercy is boundless and free.

Rev. Josiah Hopkins. 1830.

TO-DAY. 6, 4. Lowell Mason. (1792—1872.) 1831.

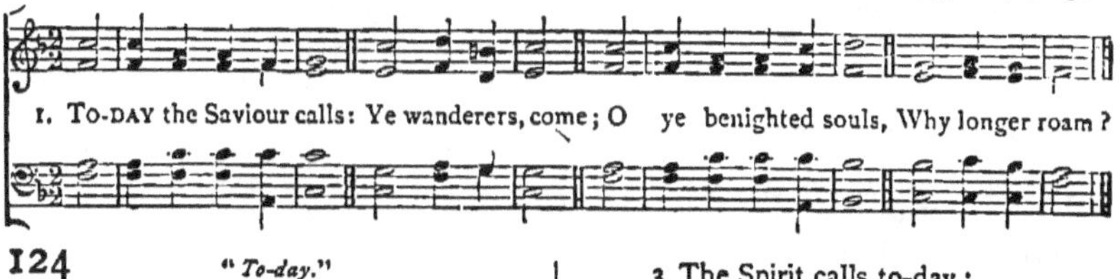
1. TO-DAY the Saviour calls: Ye wanderers, come; O ye benighted souls, Why longer roam?

124 *"To-day."*

2 To-day the Saviour calls:
O hear Him now;
Within these sacred walls
To Jesus bow.

3 The Spirit calls to-day:
Yield to His power;
O grieve him not away,
'Tis mercy's hour.

Rev. Samuel Francis Smith. (1808—). 1831 alt
Thomas Hastings, (1784—1872.) 1831.

ZEPHYR. L. M. William Batchelder Bradbury. (1816—1868) 1844.

1. BE-HOLD, a stranger's at the door: He gently knocks, has knocked be-fore;
Has wait-ed long, is wait-ing still: You treat no oth-er friend so ill.

125 *Christ knocking at the Door.*
Cant. v. 2. Rev. iii. 20.

2 But will He prove a friend indeed?
He will, the very friend you need;
The Man of Nazareth, 'tis He,
With garments dyed at Calvary.

3 O lovely attitude! He stands
With melted heart and laden hands:
O matchless kindness! and He shows
This matchless kindness to His foes.

4 Rise, touched with gratitude divine;
Turn out His enemy and thine,
That soul-destroying monster, Sin;
And let the Heavenly Stranger in.

5 Admit Him, ere His anger burn;
His feet departed, ne'er return!
Admit Him; or the hour's at hand
When at His door denied you'll stand.

Rev. Joseph Grigg. (—1768.) 1765. ab. and alt.

126 *Christ's Invitation to Sinners.*
Matt. xi. 28—30.

1 "COME hither, all ye weary souls,
Ye heavy-laden sinners, come;
I'll give you rest from all your toils,
And raise you to my heavenly home.

2 "They shall find rest that learn of Me;
I'm of a meek and lowly mind;
But passion rages like the sea,
And pride is restless as the wind.

3 "Blest is the man whose shoulders take
My yoke, and bear it with delight;
My yoke is easy to his neck,
My grace shall make the burden light."

4 Jesus, we come at Thy command;
With faith, and hope, and humble zea.
Resign our spirits to Thy hand,
To mould and guide us at Thy will.

Rev. Isaac Watts. (1674—1748.) 1709.

127 *"Asleep in Jesus."*

1 ASLEEP in Jesus: blessed sleep,
From which none ever wakes to weep,
A calm and undisturbed repose,
Unbroken by the last of foes.

2 Asleep in Jesus: O how sweet
To be for such a slumber meet;
With holy confidence to sing,
That death hath lost his venomed sting.

3 Asleep in Jesus: peaceful rest,
Whose waking is supremely blest;
No fear, no woe, shall dim that hour
That manifests the Saviour's power.

4 Asleep in Jesus: far from thee
Thy kindred and their graves may be;
But thine is still a blessed sleep,
From which none ever wakes to weep.

Mrs. Margaret Mackay. 1832. ab

HENLEY. 11, 10. Lowell Mason. (1792—1872.) 1854.

1. Come un-to me, when shadows darkly gather, When the sad heart is weary and distrest,
Seeking for comfort from your Heavenly Father, Come un- to me, And I will give you rest.

128 *Christ giving Rest.*

2 Large are the mansions in thy Father's
dwelling, [dim;
Glad are the homes that sorrows never
Sweet are the harps in holy music swelling,
Soft are the tones which raise the heaven-
ly hymn.

3 There, like an Eden blossoming in glad
ness,
Bloom the fair flowers the earth too rudely
pressed;
Come unto me, all ye who droop in sadness,
Come unto me, and I will give you rest.

Unknown Author. 1854. ab.

COME, YE DISCONSOLATE. 11, 10. Samuel Webbe. (1740—1816.) 1800.

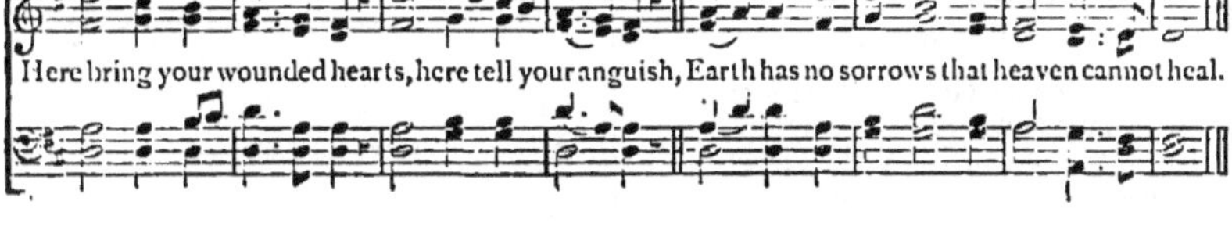
Choir.
1. Come, ye dis-con-solate, where'er ye languish, Come to the mercy-seat, fervently kneel;
Congregation.
Here bring your wounded hearts, here tell your anguish, Earth has no sorrows that heaven cannot heal.

129 *"Come, ye disconsolate."*

2 Here see the Bread of Life, see waters
flowing [above.
Forth from the throne of God, pure from
Come to the feast prepared, come, ever
knowing [move
Earth has no sorrows but heaven can re-

Thomas Moore. (1779—1852.) 1816. v. 1. alt.
Thomas Hastings. (1784—1872.) v. 2.

WOODWORTH. L. M. 54 William Batchelder Bradbury. (1816—1868. 1849.

1. God call - ing yet! shall I not hear? Earth's pleasures shall I still hold dear?
Shall life's swift pass - ing years all fly, And still my soul in slumbers lie?

130 "*Gott rufet noch.*"

2 God calling yet! shall I not rise?
Can I His loving voice despise,
And basely His kind care repay?
He calls me still; can I delay?

3 God calling yet! and shall He knock,
And I my heart the closer lock?
He still is waiting to receive,
And shall I dare His Spirit grieve?

4 God calling yet! I cannot stay;
My heart I yield without delay:
Vain world, farewell, from thee I part;
The voice of God hath reached my heart.

Gerhard Tersteegen. (1697—1769.) 1730.
Tr. by Miss Jane Borthwick. 1854. ab. and alt.

131 "*God be merciful to me a Sinner.*"

Luke xviii. 13.

1 HEAR, gracious God, a sinner's cry,
For I have nowhere else to fly;
My hope, my only hope's in Thee;
O God, be merciful to me.

2 To Thee I come, a sinner poor,
And wait for mercy at Thy door;
Indeed, I've nowhere else to flee;
O God, be merciful to me.

3 To Thee I come, a sinner weak,
And scarce know how to pray or speak
From fear and weakness set me free;
O God, be merciful to me.

4 To Thee I come, a sinner great,
And well Thou knowest all my state;
Yet full forgiveness is with Thee;
O God, be merciful to me.

5 To Thee I come, a sinner lost,
Nor have I aught wherein to trust;
But where Thou art, Lord, I would be;
O God, be merciful to me.

Rev. Samuel Medley. (1738—1799.) 1789. ab.

132 *A contrite Heart.*

Ps. li.

1 A BROKEN heart, my God, my King,
Is all the sacrifice I bring;
The God of grace will ne'er despise
A broken heart for sacrifice.

2 O may Thy love inspire my tongue!
Salvation shall be all my song;
And all my powers shall join to bless
The Lord, my strength and righteousness.

Rev. Isaac Watts. (1674—1748.) 1719. sl. alt.

EVEN ME. 8, 7.

Arr. by William B. Bradbury (1816—1868.) 1862.

1. { LORD, I hear of showers of bless-ing Thou art scattering full and free; }
{ Showers, the thirs - ty land re - fresh - ing; Let some droppings fall on me, }
E - ven me, E - ven me, Let some drop-pings fall on me.

133 "*Bless me, even me also.*" Gen. xxvii. 34.

2 Pass me not, O gracious Father,
Sinful though my heart may be;
Thou might'st curse me, but the rather
Let Thy mercy light on me,
Even me.

3 Pass me not, O tender Saviour,
Let me love and cling to Thee;
I am longing for Thy favor;
When Thou comest, call for me,
Even me.

4 Pass me not, O mighty Spirit,
Thou canst make the blind to see;
Witnesser of Jesus' merit,
Speak the word of power to me,
Even me.

5 Love of God, so pure and changeless,
Blood of God, so rich and free,
Grace of God, so strong and boundless,
Magnify them all in me,
Even me.

Mrs. Elizabeth Codner. 1860. ab.

PASS ME NOT. 8, 5.

William Howard Doane. (1832—) 1869

1. PASS me not, O gen-tle Sav - iour, Hear my humble cry; While on oth-ers Thou art
D. S. While on oth-ers Thou art
smil - ing, Do not pass me by.
call - ing, Do not pass me by.
Fine.
CHORUS.
Sav - iour, Sav - iour, Hear my humble cry,
D. S.

134 "*Pass me not.*"

2 Let me at a throne of mercy
Find a sweet relief,
Kneeling there in deep contrition,
Help my unbelief!

Mrs. Fanny Jane Crosby Van Alstyne. (1821—) 1869

DORRNANCE. (TALMAR.) 8, 7. 56 Isaac Beverly Woodbury. (1819–1858.) [illegible]

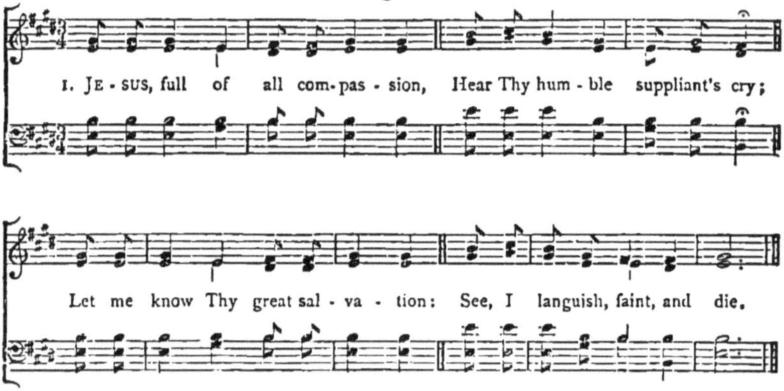
1. Je - sus, full of all com - pas - sion, Hear Thy hum - ble suppliant's cry;
Let me know Thy great sal - va - tion: See, I languish, faint, and die.

135

"*Have Mercy.*"
Mark x. 47.

2 While I view Thee, wounded, grieving,
Breathless, on the cursèd tree,
Fain I'd feel my heart believing
Thou didst suffer thus for me.

3 Hear, then, blessed Saviour, hear me!
My soul cleaveth to the dust;
Send the Comforter to cheer me;
Lo, in Thee I put my trust.

4 *Saved!*—the deed shall spread new glory
Through the shining realms above;
Angels sing the pleasing story,
All enraptured with Thy love.

Rev. Daniel Turner. (1710–1798.) 1787. ab.

136

"*Take me.*"

1 Take me, O my Father, take me,
Take me, save me, through Thy Son;
That which Thou wouldst have me, make me,
Let Thy will in me be done.

2 Long from Thee my footsteps straying,
Thorny proved the way I trod;
Weary come I now, and praying,
Take me to Thy love, my God.

3 Fruitless years with grief recalling,
Humbly I confess my sin;
At Thy feet, O Father, falling,
To Thy household take me in.

4 Freely now to Thee I proffer
This relenting heart of mine;
Freely, life and soul I offer,
Gift unworthy love like Thine.

5 Once the world's Redeemer dying,
Bore our sins upon the tree;
On that sacrifice relying,
Now I look in hope to Thee.

6 Father, take me; all forgiving,
Fold me to Thy loving breast;
In Thy love forever living,
I must be forever blest.

Rev. Ray Palmer. (1808–) 1865

ROCK OF AGES. 7. 6 l. Rev. John Bacchus Dykes. 1861.

1. Rock of a - ges, cleft for me, Let me hide my - self in Thee; Let the wa - ter and the blood,
From Thy riv-en side which flowed, Be of sin the dou-ble cure, Cleanse me from its guilt and power.

137 *"Rock of Ages."*

2 Not the labors of my hands
Can fulfill Thy law's demands;
Could my zeal no respite know,
Could my tears forever flow,
All for sin could not atone;
Thou must save, and Thou alone.

3 Nothing in my hand I bring;
Simply to Thy cross I cling;
Naked, come to Thee for dress;
Helpless, look to Thee for grace;
Foul, I to the Fountain fly;
Wash me, Saviour, or I die.

4 While I draw this fleeting breath,
When my eyelids close in death,
When I soar to worlds unknown,
See Thee on Thy judgment throne,
Rock of Ages, cleft for me,
Let me hide myself in Thee.

Rev. Augustus Montague Toplady. (1740—1778.) 1776. sl. alt.

138 *"Only Thee."*

1 Once again beside the cross,
All my gain I count but loss;
Earthly pleasures fade away,
Clouds they are that hide my day:
Hence, vain shadows! let me see
Jesus crucified for me.

2 From beneath that thorny crown
Trickle drops of cleansing down;
Pardon from Thy piercèd hand
Now I take, while here I stand:
Only then I live to Thee,
When Thy wounded side I see.

3 Blessèd Saviour, Thine am I,
Thine to live, and Thine to die;
Height or depth, or earthly power
Ne'er shall hide my Saviour more:
Ever shall my glory be,
Only, only, only Thee!

Rev. George Duffield. (1818—) 1859. ab.

TOPLADY. 7. 6 l. Thomas Hastings. (1784—1872.) 1830.

Fine.
D. C.

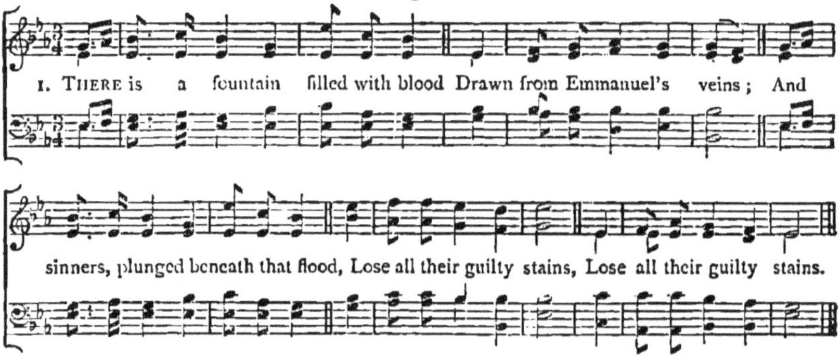
1. There is a fountain filled with blood Drawn from Emmanuel's veins; And
sinners, plunged beneath that flood, Lose all their guilty stains, Lose all their guilty stains.

139

"A Fountain opened."
Zech. xiii. 1.

2 The dying thief rejoiced to see
That fountain in his day;
And there have I, as vile as he,
Washed all my sins away.

3 Dear dying Lamb, Thy precious Blood
Shall never lose its power,
Till all the ransomed Church of God
Be saved, to sin no more.

4 E'er since, by faith, I saw the stream
Thy flowing wounds supply,
Redeeming love has been my theme,
And shall be till I die.

5 Then in a nobler, sweeter song,
I'll sing Thy power to save,
When this poor lisping, stammering tongue
Lies silent in the grave.

William Cowper. (1731—1800.) 1779.

140

Fear disarmed.

1 The Saviour! O what endless charms
Dwell in the blissful sound!
Its influence every fear disarms,
And spreads sweet comfort round.

2 The almighty Former of the skies
Stooped to our vile abode;
While angels viewed with wondering eyes,
And hailed the incarnate God.

3 O the rich depths of love divine,
Of bliss a boundless store!
Dear Saviour, let me call Thee mine;
I cannot wish for more.

4 On Thee alone my hope relies,
Beneath Thy cross I fall,
My Lord, my Life, my Sacrifice,
My Saviour, and my All.

Miss Anne Steele. (1717—1778.) 1760. ab.

141

"Vexilla Regis prodeunt."

1 The royal banner is unfurled,
The cross is reared on high,
On which the Saviour of the world
Is stretched in agony.

2 See through His holy hands and feet
The cruel nails they drive:
Our ransom thus is made complete,
Our souls are saved alive.

3 And see, the spear hath pierced His side
And shed that sacred flood,
That holy reconciling tide,
The water and the blood.

4 Hail, holy cross, from thee we learn
The only way to heaven;
And O, to thee may sinners turn,
And look, and be forgiven!

Venantius Fortunatus (530—609.) 580. ab.
Tr. by Rev. John Chandler. (1806—) 1837.

BALERMA. C. M.

Scotch Melody. Hugh Wilson. 1768.
Arr. by Lowell Mason. (1792—1872.) 1836.

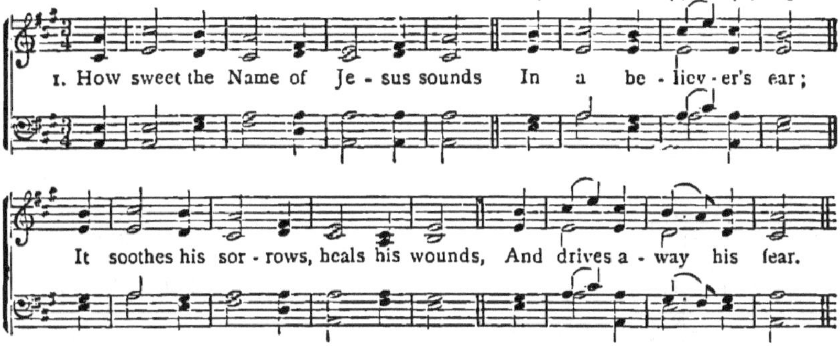
1. How sweet the Name of Je - sus sounds In a be - liev - er's ear;
It soothes his sor - rows, heals his wounds, And drives a - way his fear.

142 *The sweet Name.*

2 It makes the wounded spirit whole,
And calms the troubled breast;
'Tis manna to the hungry soul,
And to the weary rest.

3 Dear Name! the rock on which I build,
My shield and hiding-place,
My never-failing treasury, filled
With boundless stores of grace.

4 By Thee my prayers acceptance gain,
Although with sin defiled;
Satan accuses me in vain,
And I am owned a child.

5 Weak is the effort of my heart,
And cold my warmest thought;
But when I see Thee as Thou art,
I'll praise Thee as I ought.

6 Till then I would Thy love proclaim
With every fleeting breath;
And may the music of Thy Name
Refresh my soul in death.

Rev John Newton. (1725—1807.) 1779. ab.

143 *"O Deus, ego amo Te."*

1 My God I love Thee: not because
I hope for heaven thereby,
Nor yet because who love Thee not
Must die eternally.

2 Thou, O my Jesus, Thou didst me
Upon the cross embrace;
For me didst bear the nails and spear,
And manifold disgrace;

3 And griefs, and torments numberless,
And sweat of agony;
Yea, death itself; and all for me
Who was Thine enemy.

4 Then why, O blessèd Jesus Christ,
Should I not love Thee well?
Not for the hope of winning heaven,
Nor of escaping hell.

5 Not with the hope of gaining aught,
Not seeking a reward;
But as Thyself hast lovèd me,
O ever-loving Lord.

6 So would I love Thee, dearest Lord,
And in Thy praise will sing;
Solely because Thou art my God,
And my Eternal King.

Francis Xavier. (1506—1552.) 1552.
Tr. by Rev. Edward Caswall. (1814—). 1849. sl. alt.

JESUS PAID IT ALL. 7, 6. **60** William Batchelder Bradbury. (1816—1868.) 1864.

1. NOTHING, eith - er great or small, Remains for me to do; Je - sus died, and
paid it all, Yes all the debt I owe.
CHORUS.
Je - sus paid it all,......
Je - sus paid it, paid it all,
All the debt I owe, Je - sus died and paid it all, Yes, all the debt I owe.

144

"Jesus paid it all."

2 When He from His lofty throne
Stooped down to do and die,
Everything was fully done;
"'Tis finished!" was His cry.

3 Weary, working, plodding one,
O wherefore toil you so?
Cease your doing; all was done,
Yes, ages long ago.

4 Till to Jesus' work you cling,
Alone by simple faith,
"Doing" is a deadly thing,
Your "doing" ends in death.

5 Cast your deadly "doing" down,
Down all at Jesus' feet:
Stand in Him, in Him alone,
All glorious and complete.

Rev. James Procter. 1858. ab. and alt.

Always with us.

1 ALWAYS with us, always with us—
Words of cheer and words of love;
Thus the risen Saviour whispers,
From His dwelling-place above.
With us when we toil in sadness,
Sowing much and reaping none;
Telling us that in the future
Golden harvests shall be won.

2 With us when the storm is sweeping
O'er our pathway dark and drear;
Waking hope within our bosoms,
Stilling every anxious fear.
With us in the lonely valley,
When we cross the chilling stream;
Lighting up the steps to glory,
With salvation's radiant beam.

Rev Edwin H. Nevin. (1814—1853.)

NETTLETON. 8, 7. D.

Rev. Asahel Nettleton. (1783—1844) 1824.

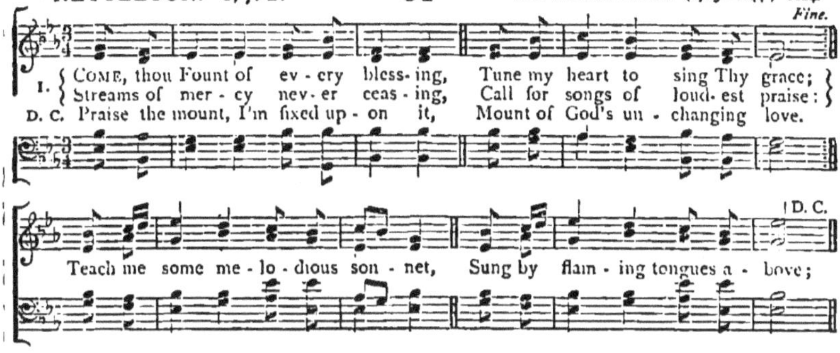
Fine.
1. Come, thou Fount of ev - ery bless - ing, Tune my heart to sing Thy grace;
Streams of mer - cy nev - er ceas - ing, Call for songs of loud - est praise:
D. C. Praise the mount, I'm fixed up - on it, Mount of God's un - changing love.
D. C.
Teach me some me - lo - dious son - net, Sung by flam - ing tongues a - bove;

145 *Grateful Recollection.*

2 Here I raise my Ebenezer,
  Hither by Thy help I'm come;
And I hope, by Thy good pleasure,
  Safely to arrive at home:
Jesus sought me when a stranger,
  Wandering from the fold of God;
He, to rescue me from danger,
  Interposed His precious blood.

3 O to grace how great a debtor
  Daily I'm constrained to be;
Let that grace now, like a fetter,
  Bind my wandering heart to Thee:
Prone to wander, Lord, I feel it,
  Prone to leave the God I love;
Here's my heart, O take and seal it,
  Seal it from Thy courts above.

Rev. Robert Robinson. (1735—1790.) 1758.

146 *"I'm a Miracle of Grace."*

1 Hail, my ever blessèd Jesus!
  Only Thee I wish to sing:
To my soul Thy name is precious,
  Thou my Prophet, Priest, and King.
O what mercy flows from Heaven,
  O what joy and happiness!
Love I much, I've much forgiven;
  I'm a miracle of grace.

2 Once with Adam's race in ruin,
  Unconcerned in sin I lay,
Swift destruction still pursuing,
  Till my Saviour passed that way.
Witness, all ye host of heaven,
  My Redeemer's tenderness.
Love I much, I've much forgiven;
  I'm a miracle of grace.

3 Shout, ye bright, angelic choir,
  Praise the Lamb enthroned above,
While, astonished, I admire
  God's free grace and boundless love.
That blest moment I received Him
  Filled my soul with joy and peace.
Love I much, I've much forgiven;
  I'm a miracle of grace.

John Wingrove.

LEBANON. S. M. D. John Zundel. (1815—) 1855

1. I was a wandering sheep, I did not love the fold; I did not love my Shepherd's voice,
D. S. I did not love my Father's voice,
Fine.
D. S.
I would not be controlled: I was a wayward child, I did not love my home,
I loved a - far to roam.

147

Lost, but found.

2 The Shepherd sought His sheep,
The Father sought His Child,
They followed me o'er vale and hill,
O'er deserts waste and wild;
They found me nigh to death,
Famished, and faint, and lone;
They bound me with the bands of love;
They saved the wandering one.

3 I was a wandering sheep,
I would not be controlled;
But now I love my Shepherd's voice,
I love, I love the fold;
I was a wayward child;
I once preferred to roam;
But now I love my Father's voice,
I love, I love His home.

Rev. Horatius Bonar. (1808—) 1844. ab.

TRUSTING. 7. William Gustavus Fischer. (1835—) 1869.

1. I am com - ing to the cross; I am poor, and weak, and blind;
Cho. I am trust - ing, Lord, in Thee, Dear.. Lamb of Cal - va - ry;
I am count - ing all but dross; I shall Thy sal - va - tion find,
Hum-bly at Thy cross I bow: Save me, Je - sus, save me now

148

2 Here I give my all to Thee,
Friends, and time, and earthly store;
Soul and body Thine to be,
Wholly Thine for evermore. *Cho.*

Rev. William McDonald. (1820—) 1869.

ORTONVILLE C. M. Thomas Hastings. (1784—1872.) 1837.

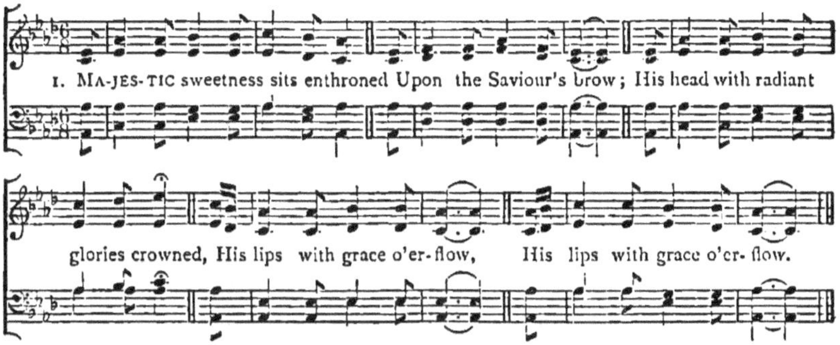
1. MA-JES-TIC sweetness sits enthroned Upon the Saviour's brow; His head with radiant glories crowned, His lips with grace o'er-flow, His lips with grace o'er-flow.

149 *"Majestic Sweetness."*

2 He saw me plunged in deep distress,
He flew to my relief;
For me He bore the shameful cross,
And carried all my grief.

3 To Him I owe my life and breath,
And all the joys I have;
He makes me triumph over death,
He saves me from the grave.

4 To heaven, the place of His abode,
He brings my weary feet,
Shows me the glories of my God,
And makes my joy complete.

5 Since from His bounty I receive
Such proofs of love divine,
Had I a thousand hearts to give,
Lord, they should all be Thine.

Rev. Samuel Stennett. (1727—1795). 1787.

150 *"A Priest forever."* Ps. cx. 4. Heb. v. 6.

1 THOU dear Redeemer, dying Lamb,
I love to hear of Thee;
No music's like Thy charming name,
Nor half so sweet can be.

2 O let me ever hear Thy voice
In mercy to me speak;
In Thee, my Priest, will I rejoice,
And Thy salvation seek.

3 My Jesus shall be still my theme,
While in this world I stay;
I'll sing my Jesus' lovely name
When all things else decay.

4 When I appear in yonder cloud,
With all Thy favored throng,
Then will I sing more sweet, more loud.
And Christ shall be my song.

Rev. John Cennick. (1717—1755.) 1745. alt.

151 *Christ precious.* 1 Pet. ii. 7.

1 JESUS, I love Thy charming name,
'Tis music to mine ear:
Fain would I sound it out so loud,
That earth and heaven should hear.

2 Yes, Thou art precious to my soul,
My Transport and my Trust;
Jewels to Thee are gaudy toys,
And gold is sordid dust.

3 All my capacious powers can wish
In Thee doth richly meet;
Not to mine eyes is light so dear,
Nor friendship half so sweet.

4 I'll speak the honors of Thy name
With my last laboring breath;
Then, speechless, clasp Thee in mine arms,
The antidote of death.

Rev. Philip Doddridge. (1702—1751.) 1755.

PRINCE. L. M. 61. Felix Mendelssohn-Bartholdy. (1809—1847.)

1. Je - sus, my Lord, my God, my all, Hear me, blest Saviour, when I call;
Hear me, and from Thy dwell-ing place Pour down the rich - es of Thy grace;
Je - sus, my Lord, I Thee a - dore, O make me love Thee more and more.

152 *"O make me love Thee more and more."*

2 Jesus, too late I Thee have sought,
How can I love Thee as I ought;
And how extol Thy matchless fame,
The glorious beauty of Thy Name?
Jesus, my Lord, I Thee adore,
O make me love Thee more and more.

3 Jesus, what didst Thou find in me,
That Thou hast dealt so lovingly?
How great the joy that Thou hast brought,
So far exceeding hope or thought!
Jesus, my Lord, I Thee adore,
O make me love Thee more and more.

4 Jesus, of Thee shall be my song,
To Thee my heart and soul belong;
All that I have or am is Thine,
And Thou, blest Saviour, Thou art mine:
Jesus, my Lord, I Thee adore,
O make me love Thee more and more.

Rev. Henry Collins. 1852.

153 *"My All in all."*

1 THOU hidden Source of calm repose,
Thou all-sufficient Love divine,
My help and refuge from my foes,
Secure I am while Thou art mine;
And lo, from sin, and grief, and shame,
I hide me, Jesus, in Thy name.

2 Thy mighty name salvation is,
And keeps my happy soul above;
Comfort it brings, and power, and peace,
And joy, and everlasting love;
To me, with Thy dear name, are given
Pardon, and holiness, and heaven.

3 Jesus, my All in all Thou art;
My rest in toil, my ease in pain;
The medicine of my broken heart;
In war, my peace; in loss, my gain;
My smile beneath the tyrant's frown;
In shame, my glory and my crown.

Rev. Charles Wesley. (1708—1788.) 1749. sl. alt.

ROCKINGHAM. L. M. Lowell Mason. (1792—1872.) 1832.

1. JE - SUS, how sweet Thy memory is! Think - ing of Thee is tru - est bliss;
Be - yond all honeyed sweets be - low Thy presence is it here to know.

154 *"Jesu dulcis memoria."*

2 Tongue cannot speak a lovelier word,
Naught more melodious can be heard,
Naught sweeter can be thought upon,
Than Jesus Christ, God's only Son.

3 Jesus, Thou Hope of those who turn,
Gentle to those who pray and mourn,
Ever, to those who seek Thee, kind,
What must Thou be to those who find?

4 Jesus, Thou dost true pleasures bring,
Light of the heart, and living Spring;
Higher than highest pleasures roll,
Or warmest wishes of the soul.

5 Lord, in our bosoms ever dwell,
And of our souls the night dispel,
Pour on our inmost mind the ray,
And fill our earth with blissful day.

Bernard of Clairvaux. (1091—1153.) 1140.
Tr. Rev. James Waddell Alexander. (1804—1859.) 1859. ab.

155 *"The Song of Songs."*

1 COME, let us sing the song of songs,
The saints in heaven began the strain
The homage which to Christ belongs:
"Worthy the Lamb, for He was slain!"

2 Slain to redeem us by His blood,
To cleanse from every sinful stain,
And make us kings and priests to God:
"Worthy the Lamb, for He was slain!"

3 To Him who suffered on the tree,
Our souls at His soul's price to gain,
Blessing, and praise, and glory be:
"Worthy the Lamb, for He was slain!"

4 To Him enthroned by filial right,
All power in heaven and earth proclaim,
Honor, and majesty, and might:
"Worthy the Lamb, for He was slain!"

5 Long as we live, and when we die,
And while in heaven with Him we reign,
This song our song of songs shall be:
"Worthy the Lamb, for He was slain!"

James Montgomery. (1771—1854.) 1853. ab. and alt.

COMFORT. 6, 9. American Melody

1. O how hap-py are they Who the Sav-iour o-bey, And have laid up their treas-ures a-bove;
Tongue can nev-er ex-press The sweet com-fort and peace Of a soul in its ear-li-est love.

156 *"How happy are they."*

2 That sweet comfort was mine,
When the favor divine
I first found in the blood of the Lamb;
When my heart it believed,
What a joy it received,
What a heaven in Jesus's name!

3 'Twas a heaven below
My Redeemer to know,
And the angels could do nothing more
Than to fall at His feet,
And the story repeat,
And the Lover of sinners adore.

4 O the rapturous height
Of that holy delight,
Which I felt in the life-giving blood!
Of my Saviour possessed,
I was perfectly blest,
As if filled with the fullness of God.

Rev. Charles Wesley. (1708—1788.) 1749. ab. and sl. alt.

I DO BELIEVE. C. M. Unknown.

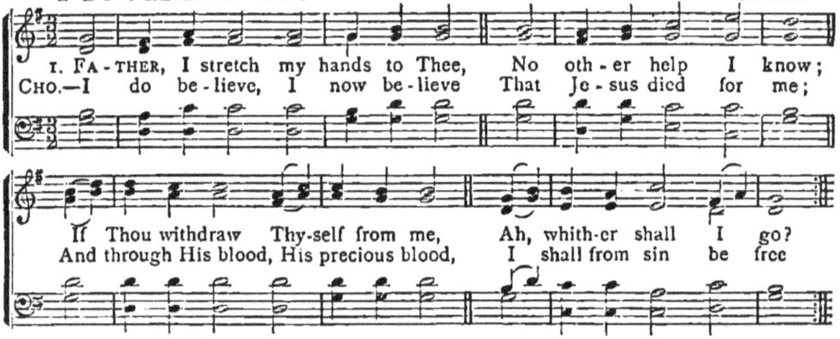
1. Fa-ther, I stretch my hands to Thee, No oth-er help I know;
Cho.—I do be-lieve, I now be-lieve That Je-sus died for me;
If Thou withdraw Thy-self from me, Ah, whith-er shall I go?
And through His blood, His precious blood, I shall from sin be free

157 *A Prayer for Faith.*

2 What did Thine only Son endure,
Before I drew my breath;
What pain, what labor, to secure
My soul from endless death! *Cho.*

3 O Jesus, could I this believe,
I now should feel Thy power;
And all my wants Thou wouldst relieve,
In this accepted hour. *Cho.*

4 Author of faith, to Thee I lift
My weary, longing eyes:
O let me now receive that gift;
My soul without it dies. *Cho.*

Rev. Charles Wesley. 1741. ab. alt. and Cho. added.

CONTRAST. *S. D.* Jonathan Edson. 1782.

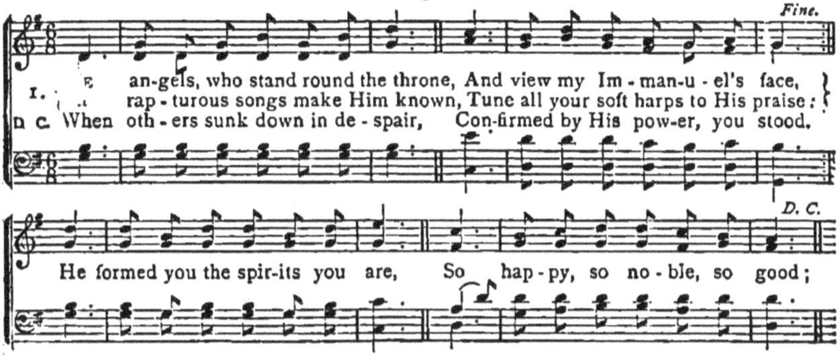
Fine.
1. an-gels, who stand round the throne, And view my Im - man-u - el's face,
rap - turous songs make Him known, Tune all your soft harps to His praise:
D. C. When oth - ers sunk down in de - spair, Con-firmed by His pow-er, you stood.
D. C.
He formed you the spir-its you are, So hap - py, so no - ble, so good;

158 *Panting for Heaven.*

2 Ye saints, who stand nearer than they,
And cast your bright crowns at His feet,
His grace and His glory display,
And all His rich mercy repeat:
He snatched you from hell and the grave,
He ransomed from death and despair;
For you He was mighty to save,
Almighty to bring you safe there.

3 O when will the period appear,
When I shall unite in your song?
I'm weary of lingering here,
And I to your Saviour belong;
I'm fettered and chained up in clay;
I struggle and pant to be free;
I long to be soaring away,
My God and my Saviour to see;

4 I want to put on my attire,
Washed white in the blood of the Lamb;
I want to be one of your choir,
And tune my sweet harp to His name;
I want, O I want to be there,
Where sorrow and sin bid adieu,
Your joy and your friendship to share,
To wonder and worship with you.

Miss Maria de Fleury. 1791.

159 *"The King in His Beauty."*

Is. xxxiii. 17, 24.

1 I LONG to behold Him arrayed
With glory and light from above,
The King in His beauty displayed
His beauty of holiest love:
I languish and die to be there,
Where Jesus hath fixed His abode;
O when shall we meet in the air,
And fly to the mountain of God?

2 With Him I on Zion shall stand,
For Jesus hath spoken the word;
The breadth of Immanuel's land
Survey by the light of my Lord.
But when on Thy bosom reclined,
Thy face I am strengthened to see,
My fullness of rapture I find,
My heaven of heavens in Thee.

3 How happy the people that dwell
Secure in the City above!
No pain the inhabitants feel,
No sickness or sorrow shall prove.
Physician of souls, unto me
Forgiveness and holiness give;
And when from the body set free,
O then to the City receive.

Rev. Charles Wesley (1708—1788.) 1762. ab

LOVING-KINDNESS. L. M Christian Lyre. 1830.

1. A-WAKE, my soul, in joy-ful lays, And sing thy great Re-deemer's praise;
He just-ly claims a song from me, His lov-ing-kind-ness, is so free,
Lov-ing-kindness, lov-ing-kindness, His lov-ing-kind-ness, is so free.

160 *"The Loving-Kindness of the Lord."* Is. lxiii. 7.

2 He saw me ruined in the fall,
Yet loved me notwithstanding all,
And saved me from my lost estate,
His loving-kindness is so great.

3 Through mighty hosts of cruel foes,
Where earth and hell my way oppose,
He safely leads my soul along,
His loving-kindness is so strong.

Rev. Samuel Medley. (1738—1799.) 1787. ab.

THE SWEETEST NAME. 8, 7. William Batchelder Bradbury. (1816—1868.) 1860.

1st. 2d. Fine.
1. { THERE is no name so sweet on earth, No name so sweet in heav-en,
The name be-fore His wondrous birth To Christ, the Saviour, [Omit...] giv-en.
D.C. For there's no word ear ev-er heard, So dear, so sweet as [Omit....] Je-sus.
REFRAIN. D.C.
We love to sing a-round our King, And hail Him bless-ed Je-sus;

161 *"No Name so Sweet."*

2 And when He hung upon the tree,
They wrote His name above Him,
That all might see the reason we
Forevermore must love Him. *Cho.*

3 So now upon His Father's throne,
Almighty to release us
From sin and pains, He gladly reigns,
The Prince and Saviour, Jesus. *Cho.*

Rev. George Washington Bethune (1805—1862.) 1858. ab.

SPANISH HYMN. 7. Spanish Melody.

Fine
1. Bless - ed Sav - iour, Thee I love, All my oth - er joys a - bove;
D. C. Ev - er let my glo - ry be, On - ly, on - ly, on - ly Thee.
D. C.
All my hopes in Thee a - bide, Thou my Hope, and naught be - side;

162 *"Only Thee."*

2 Once again beside the cross,
All my gain I count but loss;
Earthly pleasures fade away;
Clouds they are that hide my day:
Hence, vain shadows, let me see
Jesus, crucified for me.

3 From beneath that thorny crown
Trickle drops of cleansing down;
Pardon from Thy piercèd hand
Now I take while here I stand;
Only then I live to Thee,
When Thy wounded side I see.

4 Blessèd Saviour, Thine am I,
Thine to live, and Thine to die;
Height or depth, or earthly power,
Ne'er shall hide my Saviour more;
Ever shall my glory be,
Only, only, only Thee.

Rev. George Duffield, Jr. (1818—) 1859

163 *Praise to Jesus.*

1 Let us sing, with one accord,
Praise to Jesus Christ our Lord,
He hath made us by His power;
He hath kept us to this hour,
He redeems us from the grave,
He who died now lives to save;
Hearts and voices let us raise,
He is worthy whom we praise.

2 Angels praise Him, so will we,
Sinful children though we be;
Poor and weak we'll sing the more,
Jesus helps the weak and poor.
Dear to Him is childhood's prayer,
Children's hearts to Him are dear;
Hearts and voices let us raise,
He is worthy whom we praise.

Miss Dorothy Ann Thrupp. (1779-1847). 1838. ab. and alt.

164 *With Angels.*

1 Thee to laud in songs divine
Angels and archangels join;
We with them our voices raise,
Echo Thine eternal praise.

2 Holy, holy, holy Lord,
Live by heaven and earth adored;
Full of Thee, they ever cry,
"Glory be to God on high!"

Rev. Charles Wesley. (1708—1788.) 1739. ab.

ATHENS. C. M. D. Felice Giardini. (1716—1796.) 1760.

1. I HEARD the voice of Je - sus say, "Come un - to Me and rest;
Lay down, thou wea - ry one, lay down Thy head up - on my breast."
D. S. I found in Him a rest - ing - place, And He has made me glad.
Fine.
I came to Je - sus as I was, Wea - ry, and worn, and sad;
D. S.

165 *The Voice from Galilee.*

John i. 16.

2 I heard the voice of Jesus say,
  "Behold, I freely give
The living water; thirsty one,
  Stoop down, and drink, and live."
I came to Jesus, and I drank
  Of that life-giving stream;
My thirst was quenched, my soul revived,
  And now I live in Him.

3 I heard the voice of Jesus say,
  "I am this dark world's light;
Look unto Me, thy morn shall rise,
  And all thy day be bright."
I looked to Jesus, and I found
  In Him my Star, my Sun;
And in that Light of life I'll walk
  Till all my journey's done.

Rev. Horatius Bonar. (1808—) 1857. sl. alt.

166 *"Amazing Grace."*

1 AMAZING grace, how sweet the sound
  That saved a wretch like me!
I once was lost, but now am found,
  Was blind, but now I see.
'Twas grace that taught my heart to fear
  And grace my fears relieved;
How precious did that grace appear
  The hour I first believed!

2 Through many dangers, toils, and snares
  I have already come;
'Tis grace has brought me safe thus far,
  And grace will lead me home.
The Lord has promised good to me,
  His word my hopes secures;
He will my Shield and Portion be,
  As long as life endures.

Rev. John Newton. (1725—1807.) 1779.

JESU BONE PASTOR. (AMOR.) 8, 7, 6l. John Henry Willcox. (1827 –).

1. Je - sus is the Name we treas-ure; Name be - yond what words can tell;
Name of glad-ness, Name of pleas-ure, Ear and heart de - light - ing well;
Name of sweetness, pass- ing meas-ure, Sav - ing us from sin and hell.

167

Christ's Name precious.

2 'Tis the Name for adoration,
  Name for songs of victory,
Name for holy meditation
  In this vale of misery,
Name for joyful veneration
  By the citizens on high.

3 Jesus is the Name exalted
  Over every other name;
In this Name, whene'er assaulted,
  We can put our foes to shame;
Strength to them who else had halted,
  Eyes to blind and feet to lame.

4 Therefore we in love adoring,
  This most blessèd Name revere;
Holy Jesus, Thee imploring
  So to write it in us here,
That hereafter heavenward soaring,
  We may sing with angels there.

Unknown Author of the 14th and 15th Century.
Tr. by Rev. John Mason Neale. (1818—1866.) 1851. ab. and alt.

168

"Ich will Dich lieben."

1 Pet. i. 8.

1 I WILL love Thee, all my treasure;
  I will love Thee, all my strength;
I will love Thee without measure,
  And will love Thee right at length:
I will love Thee, Light Divine,
  Till I die and find Thee mine.

2 I will praise Thee, Sun of Glory,
  For Thy beams have gladness bro't;
I will praise Thee, will adore Thee,
  For the light I vainly sought;
Praise Thee that Thy words so blest
  Spake my sin-sick soul to rest.

3 I will love in joy or sorrow,
  Crowning joy! will love Thee well:
I will love to-day, to-morrow,
  While I in this body dwell;
I will love Thee, Light Divine,
  Till I die, and find Thee mine.

Johann Angelus Silesius. (1624—1677.) 1657
Tr. by Miss Jane Borthwick. 1854. ab

1. COME, we that love the Lord, And let our joys be known; Join
in a song of sweet ac - cord, And thus sur - round the throne.

169 *Heavenly Joy on Earth.*

2 Let those refuse to sing
That never knew our God;
But favorites of the heavenly King
May speak their joys abroad.

3 The men of grace have found
Glory begun below;
Celestial fruits on earthly ground
From faith and hope may grow.

4 The hill of Zion yields
A thousand sacred sweets
Before we reach the heavenly fields,
Or walk the golden streets.

5 Then let our songs abound,
And every tear be dry;
We're marching through Immanuel's ground
To fairer worlds on high.

Rev. Isaac Watts. (1674—1748.) 1709. ab.

170 *"Our Captain leads us on."*

1 OUR Captain leads us on;
He beckons from the skies;
He reaches out a starry crown,
And bids us take the prize.

2 "Be faithful unto death,
Partake My victory,
And thou shalt wear this glorious wreath,
And thou shalt reign with Me."

3 'Tis thus the righteous Lord
To every soldier saith,
Eternal life is the reward
Of all-victorious faith.

4 Who conquer in His might
The victor's meed receive;
They claim a kingdom in His right,
Which God will freely give

Rev. Charles Wesley. (1708—1788.) 1749. ab. and. sl. alt

ELLESDIE. 8, 7. D. **73** Arr. from Johann C. W. A. Mozart. (1756—1791.)

1. JE - sus, I my cross have ta - ken, All to leave, and fol - low Thee;
Des - ti - tute, des - pised, for - sa - ken, Thou, from hence, my all shalt be:
D. S. Yet how rich is my con - di - tion, God and heaven are still my own!
Fine.
Per - ish, ev - ery fond am - bi - tion, All I've sought, and hoped, and known,
D. S.

171

"We have left all."
Mark x. 28.

2 Let the world despise and leave me,
They have left my Saviour, too;
Human hearts and looks deceive me;
Thou art not, like man, untrue;
And while Thou shalt smile upon me,
God of wisdom, love, and might,
Foes may hate, and friends may shun me,
Show Thy face and all is bright.

3 Man may trouble and distress me,
'Twill but drive me to Thy breast;
Life with trials hard may press me,
Heaven will bring me sweeter rest.
O 'tis not in grief to harm me
While Thy love is left to me;
O 'twere not in joy to charm me,
Were that joy unmixed with Thee.

Rev. Henry Francis Lyte. (1793—1847.) 1825.

172

The End of Trials.
(Second part of preceding hymn.)

1 TAKE, my soul, thy full salvation,
Rise o'er sin, and fear, and care;
Joy to find in every station
Something still to do or bear.
Think what Spirit dwells within thee;
What a Father's smile is thine;
What a Saviour died to win thee:
Child of heaven, shouldst thou repine?

2 Haste thee on from grace to glory,
Armed by faith, and winged by prayer
Heaven's eternal day's before thee,
God's own hand shall guide thee there
Soon shall close thy earthly mission,
Swift shall pass thy pilgrim days,
Hope soon change to glad fruition,
Faith to sight, and prayer to praise.

Rev. Henry Francis Lyte. 1825.

RATHBUN. 8, 7. 74 Ithamar Conkey. (1815—1867.) 1851.

1. In the cross of Christ I glo - ry, Towering o'er the wrecks of time;
All the light of sa - cred sto - ry Gath - ers round its head su - blime.

173

Glorying in the Cross.
Gal. vi. 14.

2 When the woes of life o'ertake me,
Hopes deceive, and fears annoy,
Never shall the cross forsake me;
Lo, it glows with peace and joy,

3 When the sun of bliss is beaming
Light and love upon my way,
From the cross the radiance streaming
Adds more lustre to the day.

4 Bane and blessing, pain and pleasure,
By the cross are sanctified;
Peace is there, that knows no measure,
Joys that through all time abide.

5 In the cross of Christ I glory,
Towering o'er the wrecks of time;
All the light of sacred story
Gathers round its head sublime.

Sir John Bowring. (1792—1872.) 1825.

174

"God is Love."
1 John iv. 8.

1 GOD is love: His mercy brightens
All the path in which we rove;
Bliss He wakes, and woe He lightens:
God is wisdom, God is love.

2 Chance and change are busy ever;
Man decays, and ages move;
But His mercy waneth never:
God is wisdom, God is love.

3 E'en the hour that darkest seemeth
Will His changeless goodness prove;
From the mist His brightness streameth
God is wisdom, God is love.

4 He with earthly cares entwineth
Hope and comfort from above;
Everywhere His Glory shineth:
God is wisdom, God is love.

Sir John Bowring. 1825.

175

"I would love Thee."

1 I WOULD love Thee, God and Father,
My Redeemer and my King:
I would love Thee; for, without Thee,
Life is but a bitter thing.

2 I would love Thee: look upon me,
Ever guide me with Thine eye;
I would love Thee: if not nourished
By Thy love, my soul would die.

3 I would love Thee: may Thy brightness
Dazzle my rejoicing eyes;
I would love Thee: may Thy goodness
Watch from heaven o'er all I prize.

4 I would love Thee; I have vowed it:
On Thy love my heart is set;
While I love Thee, I will never
My Redeemer's blood forget.

Madame Jeanne M. B. de la M. Guyon. (1648—1717.) 1720

LOUVAN. L. M. Virgil Corydon Taylor. (1817—) 1847.

1. My gracious Lord, I own Thy right To ev - ery ser - vice I can pay,
And call it my su - preme de - light To hear Thy dic - tates and o - bey.

176

Christ's Service the Fruit of our Labors.

Phil. i. 22.

2 What is my being but for Thee,
Its sure support, its noblest end,
Thine ever-smiling face to see,
And serve the cause of such a Friend!

3 I would not breathe for worldly joy,
Or to increase my worldly good;
Nor future days nor powers employ
To spread a sounding name abroad.

4 'Tis to my Saviour I would live,
To Him who for my ransom died;
Nor could the bowers of Eden give
Such bliss as blossoms at His side.

5 His work my hoary age shall bless,
When youthful vigor is no more
And my last hour of life confess
His dying love, His saving power.

Rev. Philip Doddridge. (1702—1751.) 1755. alt.

177

Holiness and Grace.

Titus ii. 10–13.

1 So let our lips and lives express
The holy gospel we profess;
So let our works and virtues shine,
To prove the doctrine all divine.

2 Thus shall we best proclaim abroad
The honors of our Saviour God;
When His salvation reigns within,
And grace subdues the power of sin.

3 Our flesh and sense must be denied,
Passion and envy, lust and pride;
While justice, temperance, truth, and love,
Our inward piety approve.

4 Religion bears our spirits up,
While we expect that blessèd hope,
The bright appearance of the Lord,
And faith stands leaning on His word.

Rev. Isaac Watts. (1674—1748.) 1709. sl. alt.

MAITLAND. C. M. Aaron Chapin. c. 1820.

1. Must Je - sus bear the cross a - lone, And all the world go free?
No, there's a cross for ev - ery one, And there's a cross for me.

178

No Cross, no Crown.

2 How happy are the saints above,
Who once went sorrowing here!
But now they taste unmingled love,
And joy without a tear.

3 The consecrated cross I'll bear,
Till death shall set me free;
And then go home my crown to wear,
For there's a crown for me.

4 Upon the crystal pavement, down
At Jesus' piercèd feet,
Joyful I'll cast my golden crown,
And His dear Name repeat.

5 And palms shall wave, and harps shall ring,
Beneath heaven's arches high;
The Lord that lives, the ransomed sing,
That lives no more to die.

6 O precious cross! O glorious crown!
O resurrection day!
Ye angels, from the stars come down,
And bear my soul away.

G. N. Allen. vs. 1-3. 1849. alt.

179

"I am not ashamed."
2 Tim. i. 12.

1 I'm not ashamed to own my Lord,
Or to defend His cause,
Maintain the honor of His word,
The glory of His cross.

2 Jesus, my God! I know His Name,
His Name is all my trust;
Nor will He put my soul to shame,
Nor let my hope be lost.

3 Firm as His throne His promise stands,
And He can well secure
What I've committed to His hands,
Till the decisive hour.

4 Then will He own my worthless name
Before His Father's face,
And in the New Jerusalem
Appoint my soul a place.

Rev. Isaac Watts. (1674-1748.) 1709.

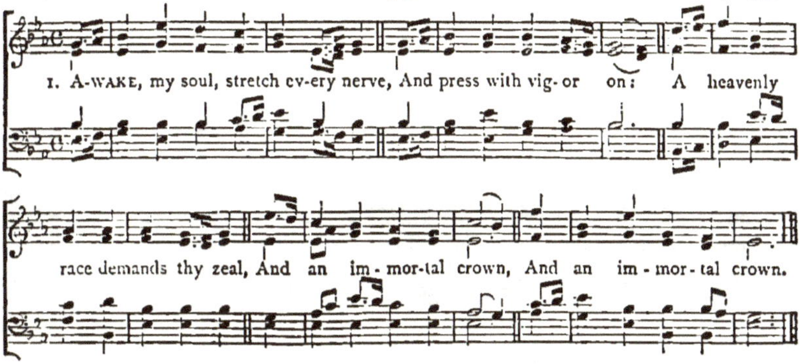
1. A-WAKE, my soul, stretch ev-ery nerve, And press with vig-or on: A heavenly
race demands thy zeal, And an im-mor-tal crown, And an im-mor-tal crown.

180 *Pressing on.*
Phil. iii. 12-14.

2 A cloud of witnesses around
Hold thee in full survey;
Forget the steps already trod,
And onward urge thy way.

3 'Tis God's all-animating voice
That calls thee from on high;
'Tis His own hand presents the prize
To thine aspiring eye:—

4 That prize with peerless glories bright,
Which shall new lustre boast,
When victors' wreaths and monarchs' gems
Shall blend in common dust.

5 Blest Saviour, introduced by Thee,
Have I my race begun;
And crowned with victory, at Thy feet
I'll lay my honors down.

Rev Philip Doddridge. (1702—1751.) 1755.

181 *"Hinder me not."*
Gen. xxiv. 56.

1 IN all my Lord's appointed ways,
My journey I'll pursue;
Hinder me not, ye much-loved saints,
For I must go with you.

2 Through floods and flames, if Jesus lead,
I'll follow where He goes;
Hinder me not! shall be my cry,
Though earth and hell oppose.

3 Through duty, and through trials too,
I'll go at His command;
Hinder me not, for I am bound
To my Immanuel's land.

4 And when my Saviour calls me home,
Still this my cry shall be,
Hinder me not! come, welcome death.
I'll gladly go with thee.

Rev. John Ryland. (1753—1825.) 1773. ab.

182 *The Hard Way.*

1 OUR journey is a thorny maze,
But we march upward still,
Forget these troubles of the ways,
And reach at Zion's hill.

2 See the kind angels at the gates,
Inviting us to come!
There Jesus, the Forerunner, waits
To welcome travelers home.

3 Eternal glories to the King,
Who brought us safely through;
Our tongues shall never cease to sing,
And endless praise renew.

Rev. Isaac Watts. (1674—1748.) 1709. ab.

LABAN. S. M. Lowell Mason. (1792—1872.) 1830.

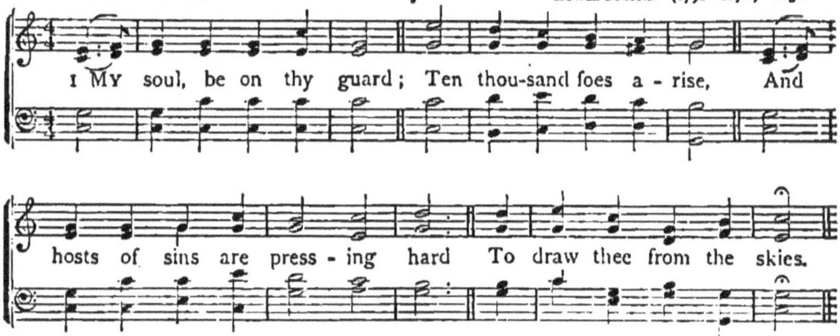
1 My soul, be on thy guard; Ten thou-sand foes a - rise, And
hosts of sins are press - ing hard To draw thee from the skies.

183 *"Be on thy Guard."*

1 My soul, be on thy guard;
Ten thousand foes arise,
And hosts of sins are pressing hard
To draw thee from the skies.

2 O watch, and fight, and pray,
The battle ne'er give o'er;
Renew it boldly every day,
And help divine implore.

3 Ne'er think the victory won,
Nor once at ease sit down:
Thine arduous work will not be done
Till thou receive thy crown.

George Heath. 1781.

184 *"Keep the Charge of the Lord."*
Lev. viii. 35.

1 A charge to keep I have,
A God to glorify,
A never-dying soul to save,
And fit it for the sky.

2 To serve the present age,
My calling to fulfill:
O may it all my powers engage
To do my Master's will.

3 Arm me with jealous care,
As in Thy sight to live,
And O Thy servant, Lord, prepare
A strict account to give.

4 Help me to watch and pray,
And on Thyself rely,
Assured, if I my trust betray,
I shall forever die.

Rev. Charles Wesley. 1762.

185 *Sowing beside all Waters.*
Is. xxxii 20.

1 Sow in the morn thy seed,
At eve hold not thy hand;
To doubt and fear give thou no heed,
Broadcast it o'er the land.

2 Thou canst not toil in vain;
Cold, heat, the moist and dry,
Shall foster and mature the grain
For garners in the sky.

3 Then, when the glorious end,
The day of God shall come,
The angel-reapers shall descend,
And heaven sing, "Harvest home!"

James Montgomery. (1771—1854.) 1825. ab.

186 *Praise to God from all nations.*
Ps. cxvii.

1 Thy name, Almighty Lord,
Shall sound through distant lands;
Great is Thy grace, and sure Thy word
Thy truth forever stands.

2 Far be Thine honor spread,
And long Thy praise endure,
Till morning light and evening shade
Shall be exchanged no more.

Rev. Isaac Watts. 1719.

CHRISTUS VICTOR. 6. 5. **79** Arr. from Sir Arthur Sullivan. 1872.

1. ONWARD, Christian sol - diers, Marching as to war, With the cross of Je - sus
Go - ing on be - fore. Christ the roy - al Mas - ter Leads against the foe;
Forward in - to bat - tle, See, His banners go..... Onward, Christian soldiers,
Marching as to war, With the cross of Je - sus Go - ing on be - fore.

187 "*Onward, Christian Soldiers.*

2 At the sign of triumph
Satan's host doth flee;
On then, Christian soldiers,
On to victory.
Hell's foundations quiver
At the shout of praise;
Brothers, lift your voices,
Loud your anthems raise.
Onward, etc.

3 Like a mighty army
Moves the Church of God;
Brothers, we are treading
Where the saints have trod;
We are not divided,
All one body we,
One in hope and doctrine,
One in charity.
Onward, etc.

4 Onward, then, ye people,
Join our happy throng,
Blend with ours your voices
In the triumph-song;
Glory, laud, and honor
Unto Christ the King;
This through countless ages,
Men and angels sing.
Onward, etc.

Rev. Sabine Baring Gould. (1834—) 1865. ab

WEBB. 7, 6. George James Webb. (1803—) 1830.

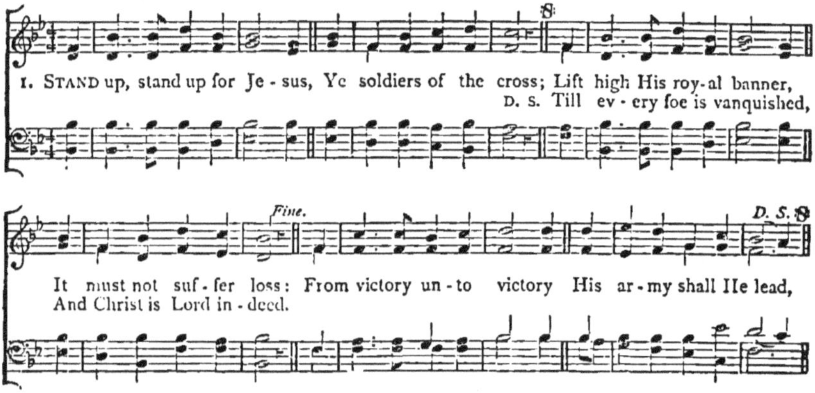
1. STAND up, stand up for Je - sus, Ye soldiers of the cross; Lift high His roy - al banner,
D. S. Till ev - ery foe is vanquished,
Fine.
It must not suf - fer loss: From victory un - to victory His ar - my shall He lead,
And Christ is Lord in - deed.
D. S.

188 "*Stand up, stand up for Jesus!*"

2 Stand up, stand up for Jesus,
The trumpet call obey;
Forth to the mighty conflict,
In this His glorious day:
"Ye that are men, now serve Him"
Against unnumbered foes;
Let courage rise with danger,
And strength to strength oppose.

3 Stand up, stand up for Jesus,
Stand in His strength alone;
The arm of flesh will fail you,
Ye dare not trust your own:
Put on the gospel armor,
Each piece put on with prayer;
Where duty calls, or danger,
Be never wanting there.

4 Stand up, stand up for Jesus,
The strife will not be long;
This day the noise of battle,
The next the victor's song:
To him that overcometh,
A crown of life shall be;
He with the King of Glory
Shall reign eternally.

Rev. George Duffield, Jr. (1818—) 1858. ab.

189 "*Go forward, Christian Soldier.*"

1 Go forward, Christian soldier,
Beneath His banner true:
The Lord Himself, thy Leader,
Shall all thy foes subdue.
His love foretells thy trials,
He knows thine hourly need;
He can, with bread of heaven,
Thy fainting spirit feed.

2 Go forward, Christian soldier,
Fear not the secret foe;
Far more are o'er thee watching
Than human eyes can know.
Trust only Christ, thy Captain,
Cease not to watch and pray;
Heed not the treach'rous voices
That lure thy soul astray.

3 Go forward, Christian soldier,
Nor dream of peaceful rest,
Till Satan's host is vanquished
And heaven is all possessed.
Till Christ Himself shall call thee
To lay thine armor by,
And wear, in endless glory,
The crown of victory.

Rev. Laurence Tuttiett. (1825—) 1854.

MENDON. L. M. German
Arr. by Lowell Mason. (1792—1872.) 1830.

1. STAND up, my soul, shake off thy fears, And gird the gos - pel ar - mor on;
March to the gates of end - less joy, Where Je - sus thy great Cap- tain's gone.

190 *The Christian Warfare.*

2 Hell and thy sins resist thy course,
But hell and sin are vanquished foes;
Thy Jesus nailed them to the cross,
And sung the triumph when He rose.

3 Then let my soul march boldly on,
Press forward to the heavenly gate:
There peace and joy eternal reign,
And glittering robes for conquerors wait.

4 There shall I wear a starry crown,
And triumph in almighty grace;
While all the armies of the skies
Join in my glorious Leader's praise.

Rev. Isaac Watts. (1674—1748.) 1709. ab. and alt.

191 *The Coming of Christ's Kingdom.*

1 ASCEND Thy throne, almighty King,
And spread Thy glories all abroad;
Let Thine own arm salvation bring,
And be Thou known the gracious God.

2 O let the kingdoms of the world
Become the kingdoms of the Lord;
Let saints and angels praise Thy name,
Be Thou through heaven and earth adored.

Rev. Benjamin Beddome. (1717—1795.) 1818. ab.

192 *The Rest that remaineth.*

1 LORD, Thou wilt bring the joyful day;
Beyond earth's weariness and pains,
Thou hast a mansion far away,
Where for Thine own a rest remains.

2 No sun there climbs the morning sky,
There never falls the shade of night,
God and the Lamb forever nigh,
O'er all shed everlasting light.

3 The bow of mercy spans the throne,
Emblem of love and goodness there;
While notes, to mortals all unknown,
Float on the calm celestial air.

4 Around the throne bright legions stand,
Redeemed by blood from sin and hell;
And shining forms, and angel band,
The mighty chorus join to swell.

5 There, Lord, Thy wayworn saints shall find
The bliss for which they longed before;
And holiest sympathies shall bind
Thine own to Thee forevermore.

6 O Jesus, bring us to that rest,
Where all the ransomed shall be found,
In Thine eternal fullness blest,
While ages roll their cycles round.

Rev. Ray Palmer. (1808—) 1865.

HE LEADETH ME. L. M. 82 William Batchelder Bradbury. (1816—1868.) 1864.

1. He lead - eth me: O blessed thought, O words with heavenly comfort fraught,
What - e'er I do, wher - e'er I be, Still 'tis God's hand that lead - eth me.
Chorus.
He lead - eth me, He lead - eth me, By His own hand He lead-eth me;
His faithful fol - lower I would be, For by His hand He lead - eth me.

193

"He leadeth me."

2 Sometimes 'mid scenes of deepest gloom,
Sometimes where Eden's bowers bloom,
By waters still, o'er troubled sea,
Still 'tis His hand that leadeth me. *Cho.*

3 Lord, I would clasp Thy hand in mine,
Nor ever murmur nor repine;
Content whatever lot I see,
Since 'tis my God that leadeth me. *Cho.*

4 And when my task on earth is done,
When, by Thy grace, the victory's won,
E'en death's cold wave I will not flee,
Since God through Jordan leadeth me.
Cho.

Rev. J. H. Gilmore. 1859.

194

The Lord our Shepherd.
Ps. xxiii.

1 The Lord Himself doth condescend
To be my Shepherd and my Friend;
I on His faithfulness rely,
His care shall all my wants supply.

2 In pastures green He doth me lead,
And there in safety makes me feed;
Refreshing streams are ever nigh,
My thirsty soul to satisfy.

3 Goodness and mercy shall to me,
Through all my life extended be;
And when my pilgrimage is o'er,
I'll dwell with Thee for evermore.

New York Dutch Reformed Collection of Psalms. 1767.

GREENVILLE. 8, 7, 4. 83 Jean Jacques Rousseau. (1712—1778.) 1750.

1 { GENT - LY, Lord, O gent - ly lead us, Pil - grims in this vale of tears, }
{ Through the tri - als yet de - creed us, Till our last great change ap - pears. }
When temp - ta - tion's darts as - sail us, When in de - vious paths we stray,
Let Thy good - ness nev - er fail us, Lead us in Thy per - fect way.

195 "*Lead us.*"

1 GENTLY, Lord, O gently lead us,
  Pilgrims in this vale of tears,
Through the trials yet decreed us,
  Till our last great change appears.
When temptation's darts assail us,
  When in devious paths we stray,
Let Thy goodness never fail us,
  Lead us in Thy perfect way.

2 In the hour of pain and anguish,
  In the hour when death draws near,
Suffer not our hearts to languish,
  Suffer not our souls to fear;
And, when mortal life is ended,
  Bid us in Thine arms to rest,
Till, by angel bands attended,
  We awake among the blest.

Thomas Hastings. (1784—1872.) 1830, 1850, 1859.

196 *The elder Brother.*

1 YES, for me, for me He careth
  With a brother's tender care;
Yes, with me, with me He shareth
  Every burden, every fear.
Yes, o'er me, o'er me He watcheth,
  Ceaseless watcheth, night and day;
Yes, e'en me, e'en me He snatcheth
  From the perils of the way.

2 Yes, for me He standeth pleading
  At the mercy-seat above;
Ever for me interceding,
  Constant in untiring love.
Yes, in me abroad He sheddeth
  Joys unearthly, love and light;
And to cover me He spreadeth
  His paternal wing of might.

3 Yes, in me, in me He dwelleth;
  I in Him, and He in me!
And my empty soul He filleth,
  Here and through eternity.
Thus I wait for His returning,
  Singing all the way to heaven;
Such the joyful song of morning,
  Such the tranquil song of even.

Rev. Horatius Bonar. (1808—) 1857.

LUX BENIGNA. 10, 4, 10. — Rev. John Bacchus Dykes. 1861.

LEAD, kindly Light, amid the encircling gloom, Lead Thou me on; The night is dark, and I am far from home;
Lead Thou me on; Keep Thou my feet; I do not ask to see The distant scene; one step enough for me.

197

"Lead Thou me on."

1 LEAD, kindly Light, amid the encircling gloom,
Lead Thou me on;
The night is dark, and I am far from home;
Lead Thou me on;
Keep Thou my feet; I do not ask to see
The distant scene; one step enough for me.

2 I was not ever thus, nor prayed that Thou
Shouldst lead me on;
I loved to choose and see my path; but now
Lead Thou me on!
I loved the garish day, and, spite of fears,
Pride ruled my will. Remember not past years!

3 So long Thy Power has blest me, sure it still
Will lead me on
O'er moor and fen, o'er crag and torrent till
The night is gone,
And with the morn those angel faces smile
Which I have loved long since, and lost awhile!

Rev. John Henry Newman. (1801—) 1833.

198

"I will fear no Evil."
Ps. xxiii. 4.

1 THE Lord is my Shepherd, no want shall I know;
I feed in green pastures, safe folded I rest;
He leadeth my soul where the still waters flow,
Restores me when wandering, redeems when opprest.

2 Through the valley and shadow of death though I stray,
Since Thou art my Guardian, no evil I fear,
Thy rod shall defend me, Thy staff be my stay,
No harm can befall, with my Comforter near.

3 In the midst of affliction my table is spread,
With blessings unmeasured my cup runneth o'er;
With perfume and oil Thou anointest my head;
O what shall I ask of Thy Providence more?

4 Let goodness and mercy, my bountiful God,
Still follow my steps till I meet Thee above;
I seek, by the path which my forefathers trod
Through the land of their sojourn, Thy kingdom of love.

James Montgomery. (1771—1854.) 1822.

PORTUGUESE HYMN. 11. 85 John Reading. (1690—1766.) 1760.

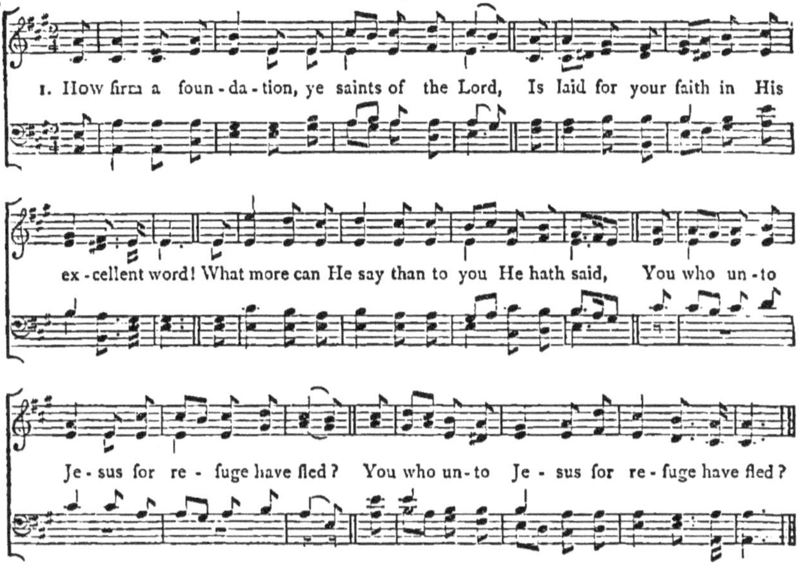
1. How firm a foun - da - tion, ye saints of the Lord, Is laid for your faith in His
ex - cellent word! What more can He say than to you He hath said, You who un - to
Je - sus for re - fuge have fled? You who un - to Je - sus for re - fuge have fled?

199

2 "Fear not, I am with thee, O be not dismayed,
For I am thy God, and will still give thee aid;
I'll strengthen thee, help thee, and cause thee to stand,
Upheld by My righteous, omnipotent hand.

3 "When through the deep waters I call thee to go,
The rivers of woe shall not thee overflow;
For I will be with thee thy trouble to bless,
And sanctify to thee thy deepest distress.

4 "When through fiery trials thy pathway shall lie,
My grace all-sufficient shall be thy supply;
The flame shall not hurt thee: I only design
Thy dross to consume, and thy gold to refine.

5 'The soul that on Jesus hath leaned for repose
I will not, I will not desert to his foes:
That soul, though all hell should endeavor to shake,
I'll never, no, never, no, never, forsake."

George Keith. 1787. ab.

ARMOUTH. 7, 6. D. Charles W. Bannister. 1822.
Arr. by Lowell Mason. (1792—1872.) 1832.

1st time.
2d time.
1. (O WHEN shall I see Jesus, And reign with Him above;)
(And from that flowing fountain..........................) Drink everlasting love! When shall I be delivered From this [vain world of
sin, And with my blessed Je-sus, And with my blessed Je-sus, And with my blessed Je-sus Drink endless pleasures in!

200 *"O when shall I see Jesus?"*

1 O WHEN shall I see Jesus,
And reign with Him above;
And from that flowing fountain
Drink everlasting love?
When shall I be delivered
From this vain world of sin,
And with my blessèd Jesus,
Drink endless pleasures in?

2 But now I am a soldier,
My Captain's gone before,
He's given me my orders,
And bid me not give o'er;
And since He has proved faithful,
A righteous crown He'll give,
And all His valiant soldiers
Eternal life shall have.

3 Through grace I am determined
To conquer though I die;
And then away to Jesus
On wings of love I'll fly.
Farewell to sin and sorrow,
I bid you all adieu;
Then, O my friends, prove faithful,
And on your way pursue.

Rev. John Leland. (1754—1741.) 1799. ab.

201 *Rejoicing in God our Saviour.*

Luke i. 47.

1 To Thee, O dear, dear Saviour,
My spirit turns for rest,
My peace is in Thy favor,
My pillow on Thy breast.
Though all the world deceive me,
I know that I am Thine;
And Thou wilt never leave me,
O blessèd Saviour mine.

2 O Thou, whose mercy found me,
From bondage set me free;
And then forever bound me
With three-fold cords to Thee;
O for a heart to love Thee
More truly as I ought,
And nothing place above Thee
In deed, or word, or thought.

Rev. John Samuel Bewley Monsell. (1811—) 1863. ab.

OLIVET. 6, 4. Lowell Mason. (1792—1872.) 1832.

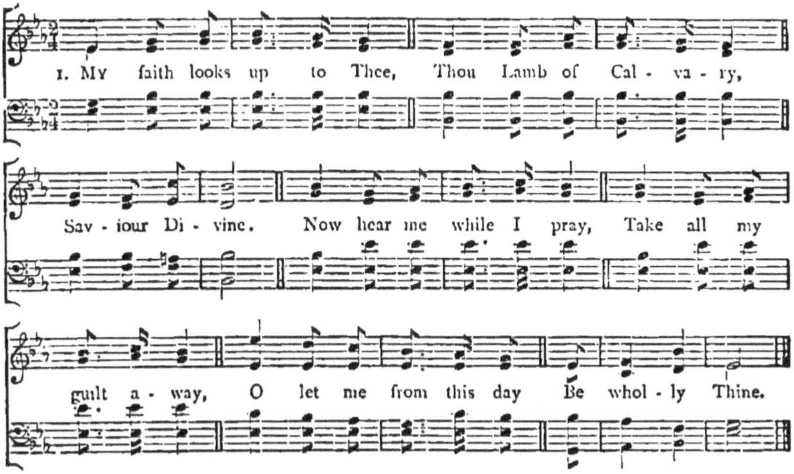
1. My faith looks up to Thee, Thou Lamb of Cal - va - ry,
Sav - iour Di - vine. Now hear me while I pray, Take all my
guilt a - way, O let me from this day Be whol - ly Thine.

202 "*My Faith looks up to Thee.*"

2 May Thy rich grace impart
Strength to my fainting heart,
My zeal inspire:
As Thou hast died for me,
O may my love to Thee,
Pure, warm, and changeless be,
A living fire.

3 While life's dark maze I tread,
And griefs around me spread,
Be Thou my Guide;
Bid darkness turn to day,
Wipe sorrow's tears away,
Nor let me ever stray
From Thee aside.

4 When ends life's transient dream,
When death's cold, sullen stream
Shall o'er me roll:
Blest Saviour, then in love,
Fear and distrust remove;
O, bear me safe above,
A ransomed soul.

Rev. Ray Palmer. (1808—) 1830.

203 "*Saviour, I look to Thee.*"

1 SAVIOUR, I look to Thee,
Be not Thou far from me,
'Mid storms that lower:
On me Thy care bestow,
Thy loving-kindness show,
Thine arms around me throw,
This trying hour.

2 Saviour, I look to Thee,
Feeble as infancy,
Gird up my heart:
Author of life and light,
Thou hast an arm of might,
Thine is the sovereign right,
Thy strength impart.

3 Saviour, I look to Thee,
Let me Thy fullness see,
Save me from fear:
While at Thy cross I kneel,
All my backslidings heal,
And a free pardon seal,
My soul to cheer.

Thomas Hastings. (1784—1872.) 15[illegible]

BETHANY. 6, 4. Arr. by Lowell Mason. (1792—1872.) 1858.

1. NEARER, my God, to Thee, Nearer to Thee: E'en though it be a cross That raiseth me;
Still all my song shall be, Nearer, my God, to Thee, Nearer, my God, to Thee, Nearer to Thee.

204 "*Nearer, my God, to Thee.*"
Gen. xxviii. 10—12.

2 Though like the wanderer,
  The sun gone down,
Darkness be over me,
  My rest a stone;
Yet in my dreams I'd be,
Nearer, my God, to Thee,
  Nearer to Thee.

3 There let the way appear
  Steps unto heaven;
All that Thou send'st to me,
  In mercy given;
Angels to beckon me
Nearer, my God, to Thee,
  Nearer to Thee.

4 Then with my waking thoughts
  Bright with Thy praise,
Out of my stony griefs
  Bethel I'll raise;
So by my woes to be
Nearer, my God, to Thee,
  Nearer to Thee.

5 Or if on joyful wing
  Cleaving the sky,
Sun, moon, and stars forgot,
  Upwards I fly,
Still all my song shall be,
Nearer, my God, to Thee,
  Nearer to Thee.

Mrs. Sarah Flower Adams. (1805—1848.) 1840.

205 "*Jesus is mine.*"

1 FADE, fade, each earthly joy;
  Jesus is mine.
Break, every tender tie;
  Jesus is mine.
Dark is the wilderness,
Earth has no resting-place
Jesus alone can bless;
  Jesus is mine.

2 Tempt not my soul away;
  Jesus is mine.
Here would I ever stay;
  Jesus is mine.
Perishing things of clay,
Born but for one brief day,
Pass from my heart away;
  Jesus is mine.

3 Farewell, mortality;
  Jesus is mine.
Welcome, eternity;
  Jesus is mine.
Welcome, O loved and blest,
Welcome, sweet scenes of rest,
Welcome, my Saviour's breast;
  Jesus is mine.

Mrs. Horatius Bonar. (1808—) 1844.

OAK. 6, 4. Lowell Mason. 1854.

1. More love to Thee, O Christ, More love to Thee! Hear Thou the prayer I make, On bended knee;
This is my earnest plea. More love, O Christ, to Thee, More love, O Christ, to Thee, More love to Thee!

206 *"More Love to Thee!"*

John xxi. 17.

2 Once earthly joy I craved,
  Sought peace and rest;
Now Thee alone I seek,
  Give what is best:
This all my prayer shall be,
More love, O Christ, to Thee!
  More love to Thee!

3 Let sorrow do its work,
  Send grief and pain;
Sweet are Thy messengers,
  Sweet their refrain,
When they can sing with me,
More love, O Christ, to Thee,
  More love to Thee!

4 Then shall my latest breath
  Whisper Thy praise;
This be the parting cry
  My heart shall raise,
This still its prayer shall be,
More love, O Christ, to Thee,
  More love to Thee!

Mrs. Elizabeth Payson Prentiss. (1819—) 1869.

207 *"Jesus is mine."*

1 Now I have found a friend,
  Jesus is mine,
His love shall never end,
  Jesus is mine:
Tho' earthly joys decrease,
Tho' earthly friendships cease,
Now I have lasting peace;
  Jesus is mine.

2 Though I grow poor and old,
  Jesus is mine;
Though I grow faint and cold,
  Jesus is mine:
He shall my wants supply;
His precious blood is nigh,
Naught can my hope destroy;
  Jesus is mine.

3 When earth shall pass away,
  Jesus is mine;
In the great judgment day,
  Jesus is mine:
O what a glorious thing,
Then to behold my King,
On tuneful harp to sing,
  Jesus is mine.

Henry Joy McCracken Hope. (1809—1872) 1852 ab.

STOCKWELL. 8. 7. **90** Rev. Darius Eliot Jones. (1815—) 1848.

1. Sav-iour, breathe an even-ing bless-ing, Ere re-pose our spir-its seal;
Sin and want we come con-fess-ing, Thou canst save, and Thou canst heal.

208 *Evening Blessing.*

2 Though destruction walk around us,
Though the arrow past us fly,
Angel-guards from Thee surround us,
We are safe, if Thou art nigh.

3 Though the night be dark and dreary,
Darkness cannot hide from Thee;
Thou art He who, never weary,
Watches where Thy people be.

4 Should swift death this night o'ertake us,
And our couch become our tomb,
May the morn in heaven awake us,
Clad in light and deathless bloom.

James Edmeston. (1791—1867.) 1820.

209 *Evening Shadows.*

1 Tarry with me, O my Saviour,
For the day is passing by;
See, the shades of evening gather,
And the night is drawing nigh.

2 Deeper, deeper grow the shadows,
Paler now the glowing west;
Swift the night of death advances;
Shall it be the night of rest?

3 Feeble, trembling, fainting, dying,
Lord, I cast myself on Thee;
Tarry with me through the darkness;
While I sleep, still watch by me.

4 Tarry with me, O my Saviour;
Lay my head upon Thy breast
Till the morning, then awake me—
Morning of eternal rest.

Mrs. Caroline Sprague Smith. 1855. ab.

210 *Desired of all Nations.*

1 Come, Thou long-expected Jesus,
Born to set Thy people free:
From our fears and sins release us,
Let us find our rest in Thee.

2 Israel's Strength and Consolation,
Hope of all the earth Thou art;
Dear Desire of every nation,
Joy of every longing heart.

3 Born Thy people to deliver,
Born a Child, and yet a King,
Born to reign in us forever,
Now Thy gracious kingdom bring

4 By Thine own eternal Spirit,
Rule in all our hearts alone;
By Thine all-sufficient merit,
Raise us to Thy glorious throne.

Rev. Charles Wesley. (1708—1788.) 1744

BOARDMAN. C. M.

Devereux.
Arr. by George Kingsley. (1811—) 1853.

1. Do not I love Thee, O my Lord? Be-hold my heart and see;
And turn each curs-ed i-dol out, That dares to ri-val Thee.

211 *"Thou knowest that I love Thee."*
John xxi. 15.

2 Do not I love Thee from my soul?
Then let me nothing love;
Dead be my heart to every joy,
When Jesus cannot move.

3 Hast Thou a lamb in all Thy flock
I would disdain to feed?
Hast Thou a foe before whose face
I fear Thy cause to plead?

4 Thou know'st I love Thee, dearest Lord,
But O, I long to soar
Far from the sphere of mortal joys,
And learn to love Thee more.

Rev. Philip Doddridge. (1702—1751.) 1755. ab.

212 *Converting Grace commemorated.*

1 O FOR a thousand tongues to sing
My dear Redeemer's praise;
The glories of my God and King,
The triumphs of His grace.

2 My gracious Master and my God,
Assist me to proclaim,
To spread through all the earth abroad,
The honors of Thy name.

3 Jesus, the name that charms our fears,
That bids our sorrows cease;
'Tis music in the sinner's ears,
'Tis life, and health, and peace.

4 He breaks the power of cancelled sin,
He sets the prisoners free;
His blood can make the foulest clean,
His blood availed for *me*.

Rev. Charles Wesley. (1708—1788.) 1740. ab

213 *"The Great Love."*
John xv. 13.

1 My blessed Saviour, is Thy love
So great, so full, so free?
Behold, I give my love, my heart,
My life, my all to Thee.

2 I love Thee for the glorious worth
In Thy great Self I see;
I love Thee for that shameful cross
Thou hast endured for me.

3 No man of greater love can boast
Than for his friend to die;
But for Thy foes, Lord, Thou wast slain
What love with Thin can vie!

4 Though in the very form of God,
With heavenly glory crowned,
Thou wouldst partake of human flesh
Beset with troubles round.

5 O Lord, I'll treasure in my soul
The memory of Thy love;
And Thy dear name shall still to me
A grateful odor prove.

Rev. Joseph Stennett. (1663—1713.) 1697. ab

OLMUTZ. S. M. Adapted by Lowell Mason. (1792—1872.) 1825.

1 BLEST are the pure in heart, For they shall see our God;
The se - cret of the Lord is theirs, Their soul is Christ's a - bode.

214 *Pure in Heart.*
Matt. v. 8.

1 BLEST are the pure in heart,
For they shall see our God;
The secret of the Lord is theirs,
Their soul is Christ's abode.

2 Still to the lowly soul
He doth Himself impart;
And for His cradle and His throne
Chooseth the pure in heart.

3 Lord, we Thy presence seek,
May ours this blessing be;
O give the pure and lowly heart
A temple meet for Thee.

Rev. John Keble. (1792—1866.) 1819. ab. and alt.

215 *Importunacy in Prayer.*
Luke xviii. 1—7.

1 OUR Lord, who knows full well
The heart of every saint,
Invites us all our griefs to tell,
To pray, and never faint.

2 He bows His gracious ear,
We never plead in vain;
Yet we must wait till He appear,
And pray, and pray again.

3 Jesus the Lord will hear
His chosen when they cry,
Yes, though He may a while forbear
He'll help them from on high.

4 His nature, truth, and love,
Engage Him on their side;
When they are grieved, His mercies move
And can they be denied?

5 Then let us earnest be,
And never faint in prayer;
He loves our importunity,
And makes our cause His care.

Rev. John Newton. 1779. ab. and alt.

NAOMI. C. M.

Hans Georg Naegeli. (1768—1836.) 1832.
Arr. by Lowell Mason. (1792—1872.) 1836.

1. FA - THER, whate'er of earth - ly bliss Thy sovereign will de - nies,
Ac - cept - ed at Thy throne of grace, Let this pe - ti - tion rise:

216 *"A calm, a thankful Heart."*

2 Give me a calm, a thankful heart,
From every murmur free;
The blessings of Thy grace impart,
And make me live to Thee.

3 Let the sweet hope that Thou art mine
My life and death attend;
Thy presence through my journey shine,
And crown my journey's end.

Miss Anne Steele. (1717—1778.) 1760. ab.

217 *"Remember me, O my God."*
Neh. xiii. 31.

1 O THOU from whom all goodness flows,
I lift my heart to Thee;
In all my sorrows, conflicts, woes,
Dear Lord, remember me.

2 When groaning on my burdened heart
My sins lie heavily,
Thy pardon speak, new peace impart,
In love remember me.

3 Temptations sore obstruct my way,
And ills I cannot flee;
O give me strength, Lord, as my day;
For good remember me.

4 Distrest with pain, disease, and grief,
This feeble body see;
Grant patience, rest, and kind relief;
Hear and remember me.

5 If on my face for Thy dear name,
Shame and reproaches be,
All hail reproach, and welcome shame,
If Thou remember me.

6 The hour is near; consigned to death,
I own the last decree:
Saviour, with my last parting breath,
I'll cry, Remember me.

Rev. Thomas Haweis. (1732—1820.) 1792.

Fine.

1. { Lord of glo - ry, who hast bought us With Thy life - blood as the price, }
{ Nev - er grudg-ing for the lost ones That tre - men - dous sac - ri - fice, }
D. C. To th' un-thank- ful and the e - vil, With Thine own un - spar-ing hand;

And with that hast free - ly giv - en Blessings count- less as the sand

D. C.

218 Acts xx. 35.

2 Wondrous honor hast Thou given
 To our humblest charity;
 In Thine own mysterious sentence,
 "Ye have done it unto Me,"
 Can it be, O gracious Master,
 Thou dost deign for alms to sue,
 Saying, by Thy poor and needy,
 " Give, as I have given to you ? "

3 Yes: the sorrow and the suffering,
 Which on every hand we see,
 Channels are for tithes and offerings,
 Due by solemn right to Thee;
 Right of which we may not rob Thee;
 Debt we may not choose but pay,
 Lest that Face of love and pity
 Turn from us another day.

4 Lord of glory, who hast bougnt us
 With Thy life-blood as the price,
 Never grudging for the lost ones
 That tremendous sacrifice,

Give us faith, to trust Thee boldly,
 Hope to stay our souls on Thee;
But, O best of all Thy graces,
 Give us Thine own charity.

 Mrs. Alderson. 1868. ab.

219 *Honoring the Lord with our Substance.* Prov. iii. 9.

1 PRAISE the Saviour, all ye nations,
 Praise Him, all ye hosts above;
Shout with joyful acclamations,
 His divine victorious love.
Be His kingdom now promoted,
 Let the earth her Monarch know;
Be my all to Him devoted,
 To my Lord my all I owe.

2 With my substance I will honor
 My Redeemer and my Lord ;
Were ten thousand worlds my manor,
 All were nothing to His word.
While the heralds of salvation
 His abounding grace proclaim,
Let His friends of every stat on
 Gladly join to spread His fame.

 Rev. Benjamin Francis. (1734—1799.) 1787. ob

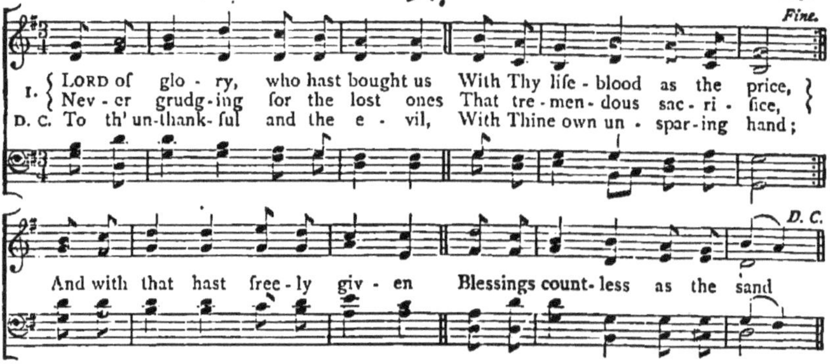

220 *"Cast thy Bread upon the Waters."*
Eccl. xi. 1.

1 CAST thy bread upon the waters,
Thinking not 'tis thrown away;
God Himself saith, thou shalt gather
It again some future day.

2 Cast thy bread upon the waters;
Wildly though the billows roll,
They but aid thee as thou toilest
Truth to spread from pole to pole.

3 As the seed, by billows floated,
To some distant island lone,
So to human souls benighted,
That thou flingest may be borne.

4 Cast thy bread upon the waters;
Why wilt thou still doubting stand?
Bounteous shall God send the harvest,
If thou sow'st with liberal hand.

Mrs. J. H. Hanaford. 1852. ab. and alt.

221 *"Closer than a Brother."*
(Abridged form.)

1 ONE there is, above all others,
Well deserves the name of Friend;
His is love beyond a brother's,
Costly, free, and knows no end.
Which of all our friends, to save us,
Could or would have shed his blood?
But our Jesus died to have us
Reconciled in Him to God.

2 When He lived on earth abasèd,
Friend of sinners was His name;
Now above all glory raisèd,
He rejoices in the same.
O for grace our hearts to soften;
Teach us, Lord, at length to love;
We, alas, forget too often
What a Friend we have above.

Rev. John Newton. (1725—1807.) 1779. ab.

222 *Giving the Heart.*

1 TAKE my heart, O Father, take it
Make and keep it all Thine own;
Let Thy Spirit melt and break it,
This proud heart of sin and stone.
Father, make it pure and lowly,
Fond of peace, and far from strife;
Turning from the paths unholy
Of this vain and sinful life.

2 Ever let Thy grace surround it;
Strengthen it with power divine,
Till Thy cords of love have bound it:
Make it to be wholly Thine.
May the blood of Jesus heal it,
And its sins be all forgiven;
Holy Spirit, take and seal it,
Guide it in the path to heaven.

Sabbath Hymn Book. 1858.

223 *"Immer muss ich wieder lesen."*

1 EVER would I fain be reading,
In the ancient holy Book,
Of my Saviour's gentle pleading,
Truth in every word and look.

2 How when children came He blessed them,
Suffered no man to reprove;
Took them in His arms and pressed them
To His heart with words of love.

3 How He healed the sick and dying,
Heard the contrite sinner's moan,
Sought the poor, and stilled their crying,
Called them brothers and His own.

4 Still I read the ancient story,
And my joy is ever new;
How for us He left His glory,
How He still is kind and true.

5 Let me kneel, my Lord, before Thee,
Let my heart in tears o'erflow,
Melted by Thy love adore Thee,
Blest in Thee 'mid joy or woe.

Miss Luise Hensel. (1798—) 1829.
Tr. by Miss Catherine Winkworth. (1829–) 1858. ab & alt

MELODY. (CHELMSFORD.) C. M. 96 Aaron Chapin. 1813.

1 How sweet, how heaven-ly is the sight, When those who love the Lord
In one an-oth-er's peace delight, And so ful-fill His word.

224 *The golden Chain.*

1 How sweet, how heavenly is the sight,
When those who love the Lord
In one another's peace delight,
And so fulfill His word.

2 When, free from envy, scorn, and pride,
Our wishes all above,
Each can his brother's failings hide,
And show a brother's love;

3 When love, in one delightful stream,
Through every bosom flows;
When union sweet, and dear esteem,
In every action glows.

4 Love is the golden chain that binds
The happy souls above;
And he's an heir of heaven that finds
His bosom glow with love.

Rev. Joseph Swain. (1761—1796.) 1792.

225 *One Church, one Army.*

1 Come, let us join our friends above
That have obtained the prize,
And on the eagle wings of love,
To joy celestial rise.

2 Let saints below in concert sing
With those to glory gone;
For all the servants of our King
In earth and heaven are one.

3 One family, we dwell in Him,
One Church above, beneath,
Though now divided by the stream,
The narrow stream of death.

4 Dear Saviour, be our constant Guide,
Then, when the word is given,
Bid Jordan's narrow stream divide,
And land us safe in heaven.

Rev. Charles Wesley. 1759. ab. and alt.

226 *The Church militant learning the Church triumphant's Song.*

1 Sing we the song of those who stand
Around the eternal throne,
Of every kindred, clime, and land,
A multitude unknown.

2 "Worthy the Lamb for sinners slain,"
Cry the redeemed above,
"Blessing and honor to obtain,
And everlasting love."

3 "Worthy the Lamb," on earth we sing,
"Who died our souls to save;
Henceforth, O Death, where is thy sting
Thy victory, O Grave?"

4 Then, hallelujah, power and praise
To God in Christ be given;
May all who now this anthem raise,
Renew the strain in heaven.

James Montgomery. (1771—1854.) 1825, 1853.

LISCHER. H. M. Friedrich Schneider. (1786—1853.) 1840

1. { WELCOME, delightful morn, Thou day of sa-cred rest: }
{ I hail thy kind return; Lord, make these moments blest; } From the low train of mor-tal toys,
I soar to reach im-mor-tal joys, I soar to reach im-mor-tal joys.
I soar to reach

227

Sabbath Morning.

2 Now may the King descend,
 And fill His throne of grace:
Thy sceptre, Lord, extend,
 While saints address Thy face;
Let sinners feel Thy quickening word,
And learn to know and fear the Lord.

3 Descend, celestial Dove,
 With all Thy quickening powers,
Disclose a Saviour's love,
 And bless these sacred hours;
Then shall my soul new life obtain,
Nor Sabbaths ere be spent in vain.

Hayward. In John Dobell's Collection. 1806.

228

Sabbath Morning.

1 AWAKE, our drowsy souls,
 Shake off each slothful band;
The wonders of this day
 Our noblest songs demand:
Auspicious morn, thy blissful rays
Bright seraphs hail, in songs of praise.

2 At thy approaching dawn,
 Reluctant death resigned
The glorious Prince of life,
 In dark domains confined:
Th' angelic host around Him bends,
And 'midst their shouts the God ascends.

3 All hail, triumphant Lord;
 Heaven with hosannas rings,
While earth, in humbler strains,
 Thy praise responsive sings:
"Worthy art Thou, who once wast slain,
Through endless years to live and reign."

Miss Elizabeth Scott. 1763.
John Dobell's Collection. 1806. ab.

229

"Take up the Strain."

1 SHALL hymns of grateful love
 Through heaven's high arches ring,
And all the hosts above
 Their songs of triumph sing;
And shall not we take up the strain,
And send the echo back again?

2 Shall they adore the Lord,
 Who bought them with His blood,
And all the love record
 That led them home to God;
And shall not we take up the strain,
And send the echo back again?

3 O spread the joyful sound,
 The Saviour's love proclaim,
And publish all around
 Salvation through His name,
Till all the world take up the strain,
And send the echo back again.

Rev. James J. Cummins. (—1867.) 1849. ab

ALVAN. 8, 7, 4. Lowell Mason. (1792—1872.) 1854

1. { In Thy name, O Lord, as - sembling, We, Thy peo - ple, now draw near: }
{ Teach us to re - joice with trembling; Speak, and let Thy ser - vants hear, }
Hear with meekness, Hear with meekness, Hear Thy word with god - ly fear.

230 *"Speak, for Thy Servant heareth."*
1 Sam. iii. 10.

2 While our days on earth are lengthened,
May we give them, Lord, to Thee;
Cheered by hope, and daily strengthened,
May we run, nor weary be,
Till Thy glory
Without clouds in heaven we see.

3 There in worship purer, sweeter,
Thee Thy people shall adore;
Tasting of enjoyment greater
Far than thought conceived before;
Full enjoyment,
Full, unmixed, and evermore.

Rev. Thomas Kelly. (1769—1855.) 1815.

231 *Dismission.*

1 LORD, dismiss us with Thy blessing,
Fill our hearts with joy and peace;
Let us each, Thy love possessing,
Triumph in redeeming grace:
O refresh us,
Traveling through this wilderness.

2 Thanks we give, and adoration,
For Thy gospel's joyful sound:
May the fruits of Thy salvation
In our hearts and lives abound;
May Thy presence
With us evermore be found.

3 So, whene'er the signal's given,
Us from earth to call away,
Borne on angels' wings to heaven,
Glad the summons to obey,
May we ever
Reign with Christ in endless day.

Hon. and Rev. Walter Shirley. (1725—1786.) 1774.

232 *For the great Congregation.*
Hab. ii. 20.

1 GOD is in His holy temple,
All the earth, keep silence here:
Worship Him in truth and spirit,
Reverence Him with godly fear;
Holy, holy,
Lord of hosts, our Lord, appear.

2 God in Christ reveals His presence,
Throned upon the mercy-seat:
Saints, rejoice, and sinners, tremble;
Each prepare his God to meet;
Lowly, lowly,
Bow adoring at His feet.

3 Hail Him here with songs of praises,
Him with prayers of faith surround;
Hearken to His glorious gospel,
While the preacher's lips expound;
Blessèd, blessèd,
They who know the joyful sound.

James Montgomery. (1771—1854.) 1853. ab

233 *Prayer for Guidance.*

1 SAVIOUR, like a shepherd lead us,
Much we need Thy tender care;
In Thy pleasant pastures feed us,
For our use Thy folds prepare.
Blessèd Jesus, Blessèd Jesus,
Thou hast bought us, Thine we are.

2 We are Thine, do Thou befriend us,
Be the guardian of our way;
Keep Thy flock, from sin defend us,
Seek us when we go astray;
Blessèd Jesus,
Hear the children when they pray.

3 Thou hast promised to receive us,
Poor and sinful though we be;
Thou hast mercy to relieve us,
Grace to cleanse, and power to free;
Blessèd Jesus,
Let us early turn to Thee.

4 Early let us seek Thy favor,
Early let us do Thy will;
Holy Lord, our only Saviour,
With Thy grace our bosoms fill;
Blessèd Jesus,
Thou hast loved us, love us still.

Mrs. Dorothy Ann Thrupp. (1779—1847.) 1838.

234 *Prayer for Guidance.*
Numbers x. 33.

1 LEAD us, Heavenly Father, lead us
O'er the world's tempestuous sea;
Guard us, guide us, keep us, feed us,
For we have no help but Thee;
Yet possessing every blessing,
If our God our Father be.

2 Saviour, breathe forgiveness o'er us;
All our weakness Thou dost know;
Thou didst tread this earth before us;
Thou didst feel its keenest woe;
Lone and dreary, faint and weary,
Through the desert Thou didst go.

3 Spirit of our God descending,
Fill our hearts with heavenly joy,
Love with every passion blending,
Pleasure that can never cloy;
Thus provided, pardoned, guided,
Nothing can our peace destroy.

James Edmeston. (1791—1867.) 1820.

235 *God giveth the Increase.*
1 Cor. iii. 7.

1 COME, thou soul-transforming Spirit,
Bless the sower and the seed;
Let each heart Thy grace inherit;
Raise the weak, the hungry feed;
From the gospel,
Now supply Thy people's need.

2 O may all enjoy the blessing
Which Thy word's designed to give
Let us all, Thy love possessing,
Joyfully the truth receive;
And forever
To Thy praise and glory live.

Rev. Jonathan Evans. (1749—1809.) 1784.

236 *Working in the Vineyard.*

1 IN the vineyard of our Father
Daily work we find to do;
Scattered gleanings we may gather,
Though we are but young and few;
Little clusters
Help to fill the garners too.

2 Toiling early in the morning,
Catching moments through the day,
Nothing small or lowly scorning,
While we work, and watch, and pray
Gathering gladly
Free-will offerings by the way.

3 Not for selfish praise or glory,
Not for objects nothing worth,
But to send the blessèd story
Of the gospel o'er the earth,
Telling mortals
Of our Lord and Saviour's birth.

4 Up and ever at our calling,
Till in death our lips are dumb,
Or till, sin's dominion falling,
Christ shall in His kingdom come,
And His children
Reach their everlasting home.

5 Steadfast, then, in our endeavor,
Heavenly Father, may we be;
And forever, and forever,
We will give the praise to Thee;
Hallelujah
Singing, all eternity.

Thomas MacKellar. (1812—) 1840.

SABBATH. 7. 6l. Lowell Mason. (1792—1872.) 1824.

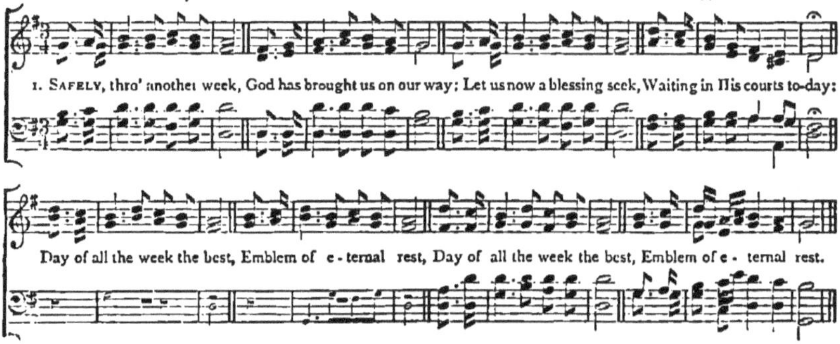
1. Safely, thro' another week, God has brought us on our way; Let us now a blessing seek, Waiting in His courts to-day:
Day of all the week the best, Emblem of e - ternal rest, Day of all the week the best, Emblem of e - ternal rest.

237 *"Safely through another Week."*

2 While we pray for pardoning grace,
  Through the dear Redeemer's name,
Show Thy reconcilèd face,
  Take away our sin and shame;
From our worldly cares set free,
May we rest this day in Thee.

3 Here we come Thy name to praise;
  May we feel Thy presence near:
May Thy glory meet our eyes,
  While we in Thy house appear:
Here afford us, Lord, a taste
  Of our everlasting feast.

4 May Thy gospel's joyful sound
  Conquer sinners, comfort saints;
Make the fruits of grace abound,
  Bring relief for all complaints:
Thus may all our Sabbaths prove,
Till we join the Church above.

Rev. John Newton. (1725—1807.) 1779.

238 *Creator, Saviour, Comforter.*

1 Great Creator, who this day
  From Thy perfect work didst rest,
By the souls that own Thy sway
  Hallowed be its hours and blest:
Cares of earth aside be thrown,
This day given to heaven alone.

2 Saviour, who this day didst break
  The dark prison of the tomb,
Bid my slumbering soul awake,
  Shine through all its sin and gloom:
Let me, from my bonds set free,
Rise from sin, and live to Thee.

3 Blessèd Spirit, Comforter,
  Send this day from Christ on high,
Lord, on me Thy gifts confer,
  Cleanse, illumine, sanctify;
All Thine influence shed abroad,
Lead me to the truth of God.

Mrs. Julia Anne Elliott. (—1841.) 1835.

RETREAT. L. M. Thomas Hastings. (1784—1872.) 1840.

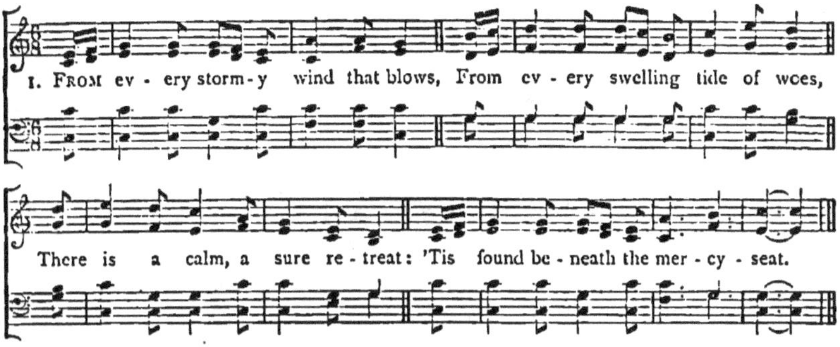
1. From ev - ery storm - y wind that blows, From ev - ery swelling tide of woes,
There is a calm, a sure re - treat: 'Tis found be - neath the mer - cy - seat.

239 *Peace at the Mercy-Seat.*

2 There is a place where Jesus sheds
The oil of gladness on our heads;
A place than all besides more sweet:
It is the blood-bought mercy-seat.

3 There is a spot where spirits blend,
Where friend holds fellowship with friend:
Though sundered far, by faith they meet
Around one common mercy-seat.

4 There, there, on eagle wings we soar,
And time and sense seem all no more;
And heaven comes down our souls to greet,
And glory crowns the mercy-seat.

Rev. Hugh Stowell. (1799—1865.) 1832. ab.

240 *"O quam juvat fratres, Deus."*

1 O Lord, how joyful 'tis to see
The brethren join in love to Thee:
On Thee alone their heart relies;
Their only strength Thy grace supplies.

2 How sweet within Thy holy place,
With one accord to sing Thy grace,
Besieging Thine attentive ear
With all the force of fervent prayer.

3 O may we love the house of God,
Of peace and joy the blest abode;
O may no angry strife destroy
That sacred peace, that holy joy.

4 The world without may rage, but we
Will only cling more close to Thee,
With hearts to Thee more wholly given,
More weaned from earth, more fixed on heaven.

5 Lord, shower upon us from above
The sacred gift of mutual love;
Each other's wants may we supply,
And reign together in the sky.

Santolius Victorinus. (1630—1697.) 1736.
Tr. by Rev. John Chandler. (1806—) 1837.

241 *On entering a new Place of Worship.*

1 Jesus, where'er Thy people meet,
There they behold Thy mercy-seat;
Where'er they seek Thee, Thou art found
And every place is hallowed ground.

2 For Thou within no walls confined,
Inhabitest the humble mind;
Such ever bring Thee where They come,
And going, take Thee to their home.

3 Dear Shepherd of Thy chosen few,
Thy former mercies here renew:
Here to our waiting hearts proclaim
The sweetness of Thy saving name.

4 Lord, we are few, but Thou art near:
Nor short Thine arm, nor deaf Thine ear
O rend the heavens, come quickly down,
And make a thousand hearts Thine own.

William Cowper. (1731—1800.) 1769. ab.

RENOVATION. S. M. Johann Nepomuk Hummel. (1778—1837.)

1 ONCE more, be - fore we part, O bless the Sav-iour's name; Let
ev - ery tongue and ev - ery heart A - dore and praise the same.

242 *At Dismission.*

1 ONCE more, before we part,
O bless the Saviour's name;
Let every tongue and every heart
Adore and praise the same.

2 Lord, in Thy grace we came,
That blessing still impart;
We met in Jesus' sacred name,
In Jesus' name we part.

3 Still on Thy holy word
Help us to feed and grow,
Still to go on to know the Lord,
And practice what we know.

4 Now, Lord, before we part,
Help us to bless Thy name:
Let every tongue and every heart
Adore and praise the same.

Rev. Joseph Hart (1712—1768.) 1762. much alt.

243 *Praise to God from all Nations.* Ps. cxvii.

1 THY name, Almighty Lord,
Shall sound through distant lands;
Great is Thy grace and sure Thy word;
Thy truth forever stands.

2 Far be Thine honor spread,
And long Thy praise endure,
Till morning light and evening shade
Shall be exchanged no more.

Rev. Isaac Watts. (1674—1748.) 1719.

244 *The Sweetness of the Sabbath.* Ps. xcii.

1 SWEET is the work, O Lord,
Thy glorious acts to sing,
To praise Thy name, and hear Thy word,
And grateful offerings bring.

2 Sweet, at the dawning light,
Thy boundless love to tell;
And, when approach the shades of night,
Still on the theme to dwell.

3 Sweet, on this day of rest,
To join in heart and voice
With those who love and serve Thee best
And in Thy name rejoice.

4 To songs of praise and joy
Be every Sabbath given,
That such may be our blest employ
Eternally in heaven.

Miss Harriet Auber. (1773—1862.) 1820. alt.

EVENTIDE. 10. William Henry Monk. 1861.

1. A-BIDE with me: fast falls the ev- en-tide; The darkness deepens; Lord, with me abide;
When oth-er help-ers fail, and comforts flee, Help of the helpless, O a - bide with me.

245 *The Eventide of Life.*

2 Swift to its close ebbs out life's little day;
Earth's joys grow dim, its glories pass away;
Change and decay in all around I see;
O Thou, who changest not, abide with me.

3 Not a brief glance I beg, a passing word;
But as Thou dwell'st with Thy disciples, Lord,
Familiar, condescending, patient, free,
Come, not to sojourn, but abide, with me.

4 Come not in terrors, as the King of kings;
But kind and good, with healing in Thy wings;
Tears for all woes, a heart for every plea;
Come, Friend of sinners, thus abide with me.

5 I fear no foe, with Thee at hand to bless;
Ills have no weight, and tears no bitterness;
Where is death's sting? where, grave, thy victory?
I triumph still, if Thou abide with me.

6 Hold Thou Thy cross before my closing eyes;
Shine thro' the gloom and point me to the skies;
Heaven's morning breaks, and earth's vain shadows flee;
In life, in death, O Lord, abide with me.

Rev. Henry Francis Lyte. (1793—1847.) 1847.

246 *Parting Hymn.*

1 SAVIOUR, again to Thy dear name we raise,
With one accord, our parting hymn of praise;
We stand to bless Thee ere our worship cease,
Then lowly kneeling, wait Thy word of peace.

2 Grant us Thy peace upon our homeward way;
With Thee began, with Thee shall end the day;
Guard Thou the lips from sin, the hearts from shame,
That in this house have called upon Thy Name.

3 Grant us Thy peace throughout our earthly life,
Our balm in sorrow, and our stay in strife;
Then, when Thy voice shall bid our conflict cease,
Call us, O Lord, to Thine eternal peace.

Rev. John Ellerton. (1826—) 1866.

247 DOXOLOGY.

All praise and glory to the Father be
And Son and Spirit, undivided Three,
As hath been alway, shall be, and is now,
To Thee, O God, the everlasting Thou.

Rev. Edward Henry Bickersteth. (1825—) 1870.

MISSIONARY HYMN. 7, 6. D. **104** Lowell Mason. (1792—1872.) 1823.

1. FROM Greenland's icy mountains, From India's coral strand, Where Afric's sunny fountains Roll down their golden sand;
From many an ancient riv-er, From many a palmy plain, They call us to de - liv- er Their land from error's chain.

248 *"From Greenland's icy Mountains."*

2 What though the spicy breezes
  Blow soft o'er Ceylon's isle,
Though every prospect pleases,
  And only man is vile:
In vain with lavish kindness
  The gifts of God are strown,
The heathen in his blindness
  Bows down to wood and stone.

3 Can we, whose souls are lighted
  With wisdom from on high,
Can we to men benighted
  The lamp of life deny?
Salvation, O salvation!
  The joyful sound proclaim,
Till each remotest nation
  Has learnt Messiah's name.

4 Waft, waft, ye winds, His story,
  And you, ye waters, roll,
Till, like a sea of glory,
  It spreads from pole t pole;
Till o'er our ransomed nature,
  The Lamb for sinners slain,
Redeemer, King, Creator,
  In bliss returns to reign.

Bp. Reginald Heber. (1783—1826.) 1819.

249 *The final Reign of Christ.*

1 WHEN shall the voice of singing
  Flow joyfully along,
When hill and valley, ringing
  With one triumphant song,
Proclaim the contest ended,
  And Him, who once was slain,
Again to earth descended,
  In righteousness to reign?

2 Then from the craggy mountains
  The sacred shout shall fly;
And shady vales and fountains
  Shall echo the reply:
High tower and lowly dwelling
  Shall send the chorus round,
All hallelujah swelling
  In one eternal sound.

James Edmeston. 1822. alt.

MELCHIOR. 7, 6 D. Melchior Teschner. 1613.

1. { Hail to the Lord's A-noint-ed, Great David's great-er Son; }
{ Hail, in the time ap-point-ed, His reign on earth be-gun. } He comes to break op-
pression, To set the captive free; To take a-way transgression, And rule in e-qui-ty.

250 "*Daily shall He be praised.*"
Ps. lxxii. 15.

2 He comes with succor speedy
To those who suffer wrong;
To help the poor and needy,
And bid the weak be strong;
To give them songs for sighing,
Their darkness turned to light,
Whose souls, condemned and dying,
Were precious in His sight.

3 He shall come down like showers
Upon the fruitful earth;
And love, joy, hope, like flowers,
Spring in His path to birth:
Before Him on the mountains
Shall peace, the herald, go;
And righteousness, in fountains,
From hill to valley flow.

4 O'er every foe victorious
He on His throne shall rest,
From age to age more glorious,
All-blessing and all-blest:
The tide of time shall never
His covenant remove;
His name shall stand forever,
That name to us is Love.

James Montgomery. (1771—1854.) 1822. ab.

251 "*The Gospel Banner.*"

1 Now be the Gospel banner
In every land unfurled,
And be the shout "Hosanna!"
Re-echoed through the world:
Till every isle and nation,
Till every tribe and tongue,
Receive the great salvation,
And join the happy throng.

2 What though th' embattled legions
Of earth and hell combine?
His power, throughout their regions,
Shall soon resplendent shine:
Ride on, O Lord, victorious,
Immanuel, Prince of peace:
Thy triumph shall be glorious,
Thine empire still increase.

3 Yes, Thou shalt reign forever,
O Jesus, King of kings:
Thy light, Thy love, Thy favor,
Each ransomed captive sings.
The isles for Thee are waiting,
The deserts learn thy praise,
The hills and valleys greeting,
The song responsive raise.

Thomas Hastings. (1784—1872.) 1832

ELTHAM. 7. D. Lowell Mason. (1792—1872.) 1840.

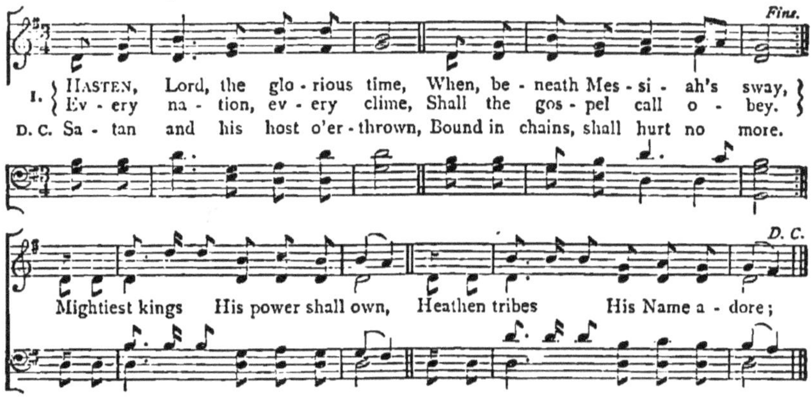
Fine.
1. { HASTEN, Lord, the glo - rious time, When, be - neath Mes - si - ah's sway,
Ev - ery na - tion, ev - ery clime, Shall the gos - pel call o - bey. }
D. C. Sa - tan and his host o'er - thrown, Bound in chains, shall hurt no more.
D. C.
Mightiest kings His power shall own, Heathen tribes His Name a - dore;

252 *The Victory anticipated.*
Ps. lxxii.

2 Then shall wars and tumults cease,
Then be banished grief and pain;
Righteousness, and joy, and peace,
Undisturbed shall ever reign.
Time shall sun and moon obscure,
Seas be dried, and rocks be riven,
But His reign shall still endure,
Endless as the days of Heaven.

Miss Harriet Auber. (1773—1862.) 1829. ab.

253 *Christ reigning over all the Earth.*

1 WAKE the song of jubilee;
Let it echo o'er the sea:
Now is come the promised hour;
Jesus reigns with glorious power.

2 All ye nations, join and sing,
Praise your Saviour, praise your King;
Let it sound from shore to shore,
"Jesus reigns for evermore!"

3 Hark, the desert lands rejoice;
And the islands join their voice:
Joy! the whole creation sings,
"Jesus is the King of kings!"

Rev. Leonard Bacon. (1802—) 1833.

254 *"The Song of Jubilee."*

1 HARK, the song of jubilee,
Loud as mighty thunders roar,
Or the fullness of the sea,
When it breaks upon the shore:
Hallelujah! for the Lord
God omnipotent shall reign;
Hallelujah! let the word
Echo round the earth and main.

2 Hallelujah! hark, the sound,
From the centre to the skies,
Wakes above, beneath, around,
All creation's harmonies.
See Jehovah's banners furled,
Sheathed His sword: He speaks; 'tis done,
And the kingdoms of this world
Are the kingdoms of His Son.

3 He shall reign from pole to pole
With illimitable sway;
He shall reign, when like a scroll
Yonder heavens have passed away:
Then the end; beneath His rod
Man's last enemy shall fall:
Hallelujah! Christ in God,
God in Christ, is All in all.

James Montgomery. (1771—1854). 1819, 1825.

John Bull ? (1563—1628.) 1605.
Henry Carey. (1693—1743.)

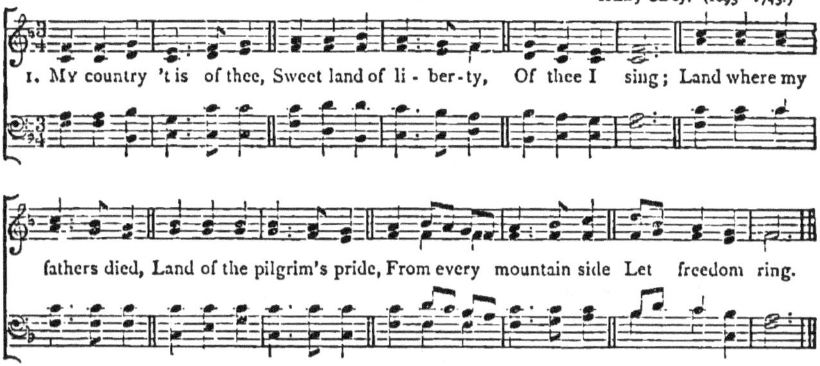
1. My country 't is of thee, Sweet land of li - ber - ty, Of thee I sing; Land where my
fathers died, Land of the pilgrim's pride, From every mountain side Let freedom ring.

255 *National Hymn.*

2 My native country, thee,
Land of the noble, free,
Thy name I love;
I love thy rocks and rills,
Thy woods and templed hills;
My heart with rapture thrills
Like that above.

3 Let music swell the breeze
And ring from all the trees
Sweet freedom's song:
Let mortal tongues awake,
Let all that breathe partake,
Let rocks their silence break,
The sound prolong.

4 Our father's God, to Thee,
Author of liberty,
To Thee we sing:
Long may our land be bright
With freedom's holy light;
Protect us by Thy might,
Great God, our King.

Rev. Samuel Francis Smith. (1808—) 1832.

256 *"God save the State."*

1 God bless our native land;
Firm may she ever stand,
Through storm and night;
When the wild tempests rave,
Ruler of wind and wave,
Do Thou our country save
By Thy great might.

2 For her our prayer shall rise
To God, above the skies;
On Him we wait;
Thou who art ever nigh,
Guarding with watchful eye,
To Thee aloud we cry,
God save the State.

Rev. John Sullivan Dwight. (1812—) 1844.

257 *Thanksgiving for Harvest.*

1 The God of harvest praise,
In loud thanksgivings, raise
Hand, heart, and voice;
The valleys laugh and sing,
Forests and mountains ring,
The plains their tribute bring,
The streams rejoice.

2 The God of harvest praise;
Hands, hearts, and voices raise
With one accord;
From field to garner throng,
Bearing your sheaves along,
And in your harvest song
Bless ye the Lord.

James Montgomery. (1771—1854.) 1822. ab. and alt.

1. { O'ER the gloom-y hills of dark-ness, Look, my soul, be still and gaze; }
{ All the prom-is-es do tra-vail With a glo-rious day of grace. }
Blessed ju-bi-lee, Blessed ju-bi-lee, Let thy glo-rious morn-ing dawn.

258

Light in the Darkness.

Matt. iv. 16.

2 Kingdoms wide that sit in darkness,
Grant them, Lord, Thy glorious light,
And from eastern coast to western
May the morning chase the night:
And redemption,
Freely purchased, win the day.

3 Fly abroad, eternal Gospel,
Win and conquer, never cease:
May thy lasting wide dominions
Multiply, and still increase:
May thy sceptre
Sway the enlightened world around.

Rev. William Williams. (1717—1791.) 1772. ab. and alt.

259

The Heathen call us.

1 SOULS in heathen darkness lying,
Where no light has broken through,
Souls that Jesus bought by dying,
Whom His soul in travail knew:
Thousand voices
Call us o'er the waters blue.

2 Christians, hearken: none has taught them
Of His love so deep and dear;
Of the precious price that bought them
Of the nail, the thorn, the spear;
Ye who know Him,
Guide them from their darkness drear.

3 Haste, O haste, and spread the tidings
Wide to earth's remotest strand;
Let no brother's bitter chidings
Rise against us when we stand
In the judgment,
From some far, forgotten land.

4 Lo, the hills for harvest whiten,
All along each distant shore;
Seaward far the islands brighten;
Light of nations, lead us o'er;
When we seek them,
Let Thy Spirit go before.

Mrs. Cecil Frances Alexander, 1850. alt.

SILOAM. C. M. 109 Isaac Beverly Woodbury. (1819—1858.) 1842.

1. SHINE on our souls, e - ter - nal God, With rays of beau - ty shine:
O let Thy fa - vor crown our days, And all their round be Thine.

260 *God's blessing invoked.*

Ps. xc. 17.

2 Did we not raise our hands to Thee,
Our hands might toil in vain;
Small joy success itself could give,
If Thou Thy love restrain.

3 With Thee let every week begin,
With Thee each day be spent;
For Thee each fleeting hour improved,
Since each by Thee is lent.

4 Thus cheer us through this desert road,
Till all our labors cease;
And Heaven refresh our weary souls
With everlasting peace.

Rev. Philip Doddridge. (1702—1751.) 1755.

261 *Christ a Pattern for Children.*

Luke ii. 40.

1 BY cool Siloam's shady rill
How sweet the lily grows!
How sweet the breath beneath the hill
Of Sharon's dewy rose!

2 Lo, such the child whose early feet
The paths of peace have trod;
Whose secret heart with influence sweet,
Is upward drawn to God.

3 O Thou, whose infant feet were found
Within Thy Father's shrine,
Whose years, with changeless virtue crowned,
Were all alike divine;

4 Dependent on Thy bounteous breath,
We seek Thy grace alone,
In childhood, manhood, age, and death,
To keep us still Thine own.

Bp. Reginald Heber. (1783—1826.) 1812.

262 *The Shepherd of Israel.*

Ps. lxxx. 1.

1 SHEPHERD of Israel, from above
Thy feeble flock behold;
And never let us lose Thy love,
Nor wander from Thy fold.

2 Thou wilt not cast Thy lambs away;
Thy hand is ever near,
To guide them lest they go astray,
And keep them safe from fear.

3 Guide us through life; and when at last
We enter into rest,
Thy tender arms around us cast,
And fold us to Thy breast.

Rev. William Hiley Bathurst. (1796—) 1831. ab

CARINA. *C. M. Double.* 110 Christian Heinrich Rink. (1770—1846.)
Arr. by George Frederick Root. (1820—) 1849.

1 THERE is a glo - rious world of light A - bove the star - ry sky,
Where saints de - part - ed, clothed n white, A - dore the Lord most high.
2 And hark, a - mid the sa - cred songs Those heaven - ly voi - ces raise,
Ten thou - sand thou - sand in - fant tongues U - nite in per - fect praise.

263 *Infant Tongues in Heaven.*

1 THERE is a glorious world of light
  Above the starry sky,
Where saints departed, clothed in white,
  Adore the Lord most high.

2 And hark, amid the sacred songs
  Those heavenly voices raise,
Ten thousand thousand infant tongues
  Unite in perfect praise.

3 Those are the hymns that we shall know,
  If Jesus we obey;
That is the place where we shall go,
  If found in wisdom's way.

4 Great God, impress the serious thought
  This day on every breast,
That both the teachers and the taught
  May enter to Thy rest.

Miss Jane Taylor. (1783—1814.) 1809.

264 *Heavenly Hope.*

1 WHEN I can read my title clear
  To mansions in the skies,
I'll bid farewell to every fear,
  And wipe my weeping eyes.

2 Should earth against my soul engage,
  And hellish darts be hurled,
Then I can smile at Satan's rage,
  And face a frowning world.

3 Let cares like a wild deluge come,
  And storms of sorrow fall;
May I but safely reach my home,
  My God, my heaven, my all:

4 There shall I bathe my weary soul
  In seas of heavenly rest,
And not a wave of trouble roll
  Across my peaceful breast.

Rev. Isaac Watts. (1674—1748.) 1709

265 *The Sweet Fields.*

1 THERE is a land of pure delight,
Where saints immortal reign;
Infinite day excludes the night,
And pleasures banish pain.
There, everlasting spring abides,
And never withering flowers:
Death, like a narrow sea, divides
This heavenly land from ours.

2 Sweet fields beyond the swelling flood
Stand dressed in living green;
So to the Jews old Canaan stood,
While Jordan rolled between.
But timorous mortals start and shrink
To cross this narrow sea,
And linger shivering on the brink,
And fear to launch away.

3 O could we make our doubts remove,
Those gloomy doubts that rise,
And see the Canaan that we love
With unbeclouded eyes;
Could we but climb where Moses stood,
And view the landscape o'er,
Not Jordan's stream, nor death's cold flood,
Should fright us from the shore.

Rev. Isaac Watts. 1709.

266 *"Jerusalem, my happy Home."*

1 JERUSALEM, my happy home,
Name ever dear to me,
When shall my labors have an end
In joy, and peace, and thee?

2 When shall these eyes thy heaven-built walls
And pearly gates behold;
Thy bulwarks with salvation strong,
And streets of shining gold?

3 O when, thou City of my God,
Shall I thy courts ascend,
Where congregations ne'er break up
And Sabbaths have no end?

4 There happier bowers than Eden's bloom
Nor sin nor sorrow know:
Blest seats, through rude and stormy scenes
I onward press to you.

5 Apostles, martyrs, prophets, there
Around my Saviour stand;
And soon my friends in Christ below
Will join the glorious band.

6 Jerusalem, my happy home,
My soul still pants for thee;
Then shall my labors have an end
When I thy joys shall see.

Unknown. Williams and Boden's Collection. 1801. ab

267 *The Promised Land.*

1 ON Jordan's rugged banks I stand,
And cast a wishful eye,
To Canaan's fair and happy land,
Where my possessions lie.

2 O the transporting, rapturous scene
That rises to my sight;
Sweet fields arrayed in living green,
And rivers of delight.

3 All o'er those wide-extended plains
Shines one eternal day;
There God, the Son, forever reigns,
And scatters night away.

4 No chilling winds or poisonous breath
Can reach that healthful shore;
Sickness and sorrow, pain and death,
Are felt and feared no more.

5 When shall I reach that happy place,
And be forever blest?
When shall I see my Father's face,
And in His bosom rest?

6 Filled with delight, my raptured soul
Can here no longer stay;
Though Jordan's waves around me roll,
Fearless I'd launch away.

Rev. Samuel Stennett (1727—1795.) 1787. ab

EVAN. C. M. **112** Arr. by Rev. W. H Havergal. (1793—1870.) 1849.

1. DEAR Je - sus, ev - er at my side, How lov - ing must Thou be,
To leave Thy home in heaven to guard A lit - tle child like me.

268 *Jesus watching over Children.*

2 I cannot feel Thee touch my hand,
With pressure light and mild,
To check me as my mother did,
When I was but a child.

3 But I have felt Thee in my thoughts,
Rebuking sin for me;
And, when my heart loves God, I know
The sweetness is from Thee.

4 And when, dear Saviour, I kneel down,
Morning and night, to prayer,
Something there is within my heart
Which tells me Thou art there.

5 Yes, when I pray, Thou prayest too:
Thy prayer is all for me;
But when I sleep, Thou sleepest not,
But watchest patiently.

Rev. Frederick Wm. Faber. (1814—1863.) 1849. ab. and alt.

269 *"Speak gently."*

1 SPEAK gently: it is better far
To rule by love than fear;
Speak gently: let no harsh word mar
The good we may do here.

2 Speak gently to the little child:
Its love be sure to gain;
Teach it in accents soft and mild;
It may not long remain.

3 Speak gently to the young: for they
Will have enough to bear;
Pass through this life as best they may,
'Tis full of anxious care.

4 Speak gently to the aged one,
Grieve not the care-worn heart:
The sands of life are nearly run,
Let them in peace depart.

5 Speak gently to the erring: know
They must have toiled in vain;
Perchance unkindness made them so;
O win them back again.

6 Speak gently: 'tis a little thing,
Dropped in the heart's deep well;
The good, the joy, that it may bring,
Eternity shall tell.

George Washington Hangford. 1841. ab.

ST. SYLVESTER. 8, 7. Rev. John Bacchus Dykes. 1861.

1. JE - SUS, ten - der Shepherd, hear me, Bless Thy lit - tle lamb to - night;
Through the dark - ness be Thou near me, Keep me safe till morn - ing light.

270 *Child's Evening Prayer.*

2 All this day Thy hand has led me,
And I thank Thee for Thy care;
Thou hast clothed me, warmed and fed me,
Listen to my evening prayer.

3 Let my sins be all forgiven,
Bless the friends I love so well;.
Take me when I die to heaven,
Happy there with Thee to dwell.

Mrs. Mary Lundie Duncan. (1814—1840.) 1839.

271 *Christ's Example.*

1 JESUS Christ, my Lord and Saviour,
Once became a child like me;
O that in my whole behavior,
He my pattern still might be.

2 All my nature is unholy,
Pride and passion dwell within;
But the Lord was meek and lowly,
Pure and spotless, free from sin.

3 While I'm often vainly trying
Some new pleasure to possess,
He was always self-denying,
Patient in His worst distress.

4 Let me never be forgetful
Of His precepts any more;
Idle, passionate, and fretful,
As I've often been before.

5 Lord, though now Thou art in glory,
We have Thine example still;
I can read Thy sacred story,
And obey Thy holy will.

6 Help me by that rule to measure
Every word and every thought,
Thinking it my greatest pleasure
There to learn what Thou hast taught.

Miss Jane Taylor. (1783—1824.) 1800.

272 *Christ's great Love and Condescension.*

1 WHAT a strange and wondrous story,
From the Book of God is read:
How the Lord of life and glory
Had not where to lay His head.

2 How He left His throne in heaven,
Here to suffer, bleed, and die,
That my soul might be forgiven,
And ascend to God on high.

3 Father, let Thy Holy Spirit
Still reveal a Saviour's love,
And prepare me to inherit
Glory where He reigns above;

4 There, with saints and angels dwelling,
May I that great love proclaim,
And with them be ever telling
All the wonders of His name.

Miss Dorothy Ann Thrupp. (1779—1847.) 1830.

AROUND THE THRONE. C. M. English. Arr. by H. E. Matthews. 1841.

1. AROUND the throne of God in heaven, Thousands of children stand; Children whose sins are
all forgiven, A ho - ly, happy band, Singing, Glory, glo-ry, glo-ry be to God on high.
CHORUS.

273 *Children around God's Throne.* Rev. vii. 13.

2 In flowing robes of spotless white
See every one arrayed;
Dwelling in everlasting light,
And joys that never fade. *Cho.*

3 What brought them to that world above,
That heaven so bright and fair,
Where all is peace, and joy, and love;
How came those children there? *Cho.*

4 Because the Saviour shed His blood,
To wash away their sin;
Bathed in that pure and precious flood,
Behold them white and clean. *Cho.*

5 On earth they sought the Saviour's grace,
On earth they loved His name;
So now they see His blessèd face,
And stand before the Lamb. *Cho.*

Mrs. Anne Houlditch Shepherd. (1809—1857.) 1841. ab.

I'M A PILGRIM. 9, 11, 10, 10. German Melody.

Fine.
D. C.
1. I'm a pilgrim, and I'm a stranger; I can tarry, I can tarry, but a night;
D. C. I'm a pilgrim, &c.
Do not detain me, for I am go - ing
To where the fountains are ever flowing:

274 *"Strangers and Pilgrims."* Heb. xi. 13.

2 There the glory is ever shining:
O, my longing heart, my longing heart is
there;
Here in this country so dark and dreary,
I long have wandered forlorn and weary.

3 There's the city to which I journey;
My Redeemer, my Redeemer is its light;
There is no sorrow, nor any sighing,
Nor any tears there, nor any dying.

Mrs. Mary S. B. Dana. (1810—) 1840.

SWEET HOUR OF PRAYER. L. M. D. 115 William Batchelder Bradbury. (1816—1868.) 1859.

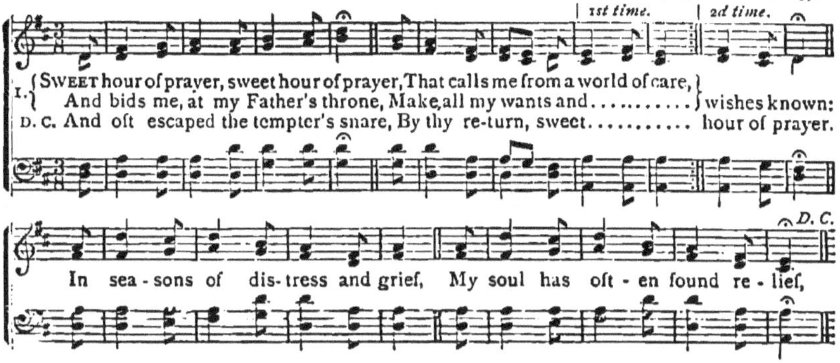
1st time.
2d time.
1. Sweet hour of prayer, sweet hour of prayer, That calls me from a world of care,
And bids me, at my Father's throne, Make all my wants and .... wishes known:
D. C. And oft escaped the tempter's snare, By thy re-turn, sweet .... hour of prayer.
D. C.
In sea-sons of dis-tress and grief, My soul has oft-en found re-lief,

275 *"Sweet Hour of Prayer."*

2 Sweet hour of prayer, sweet hour of prayer,
Thy wings shall my petition bear
To Him whose truth and faithfulness
Engage the waiting soul to bless:
And since He bids me seek His face,
Believe His word, and trust His grace,
I'll cast on Him my every care,
And wait for thee, sweet hour of prayer.

3 Sweet hour of prayer, sweet hour of prayer,
May I thy consolation share,
Till from Mount Pisgah's lofty height,
I view my home and take my flight:
This robe of flesh I'll drop, and rise
To seize the everlasting prize;
And shout, while passing through the air,
Farewell, farewell, sweet hour of prayer.

Rev. W. W. Walford. 1846.

276 *Evening Prayer for Healing.*

Mark i. 32.

1 At even, ere the sun was set,
The sick, O Lord, around Thee lay;
O in what divers pains they met,
O with what joy they went away.
Once more 'tis eventide, and we,
Oppressed with various ills, draw near;
What if Thy form we cannot see?
We know and feel that Thou art here.

2 O Saviour Christ, our woes dispel,
For some are sick, and some are sad,
And some have never loved Thee well,
And some have lost the love they had;
And none, O Lord, have perfect rest,
For none are wholly free from sin;
And they who fain would serve Thee best,
Are conscious most of wrong within.

3 O Saviour Christ, Thou too art Man;
Thou hast been troubled, tempted, tried
Thy kind but searching glance can scan
The very wounds that shame would hide
Thy touch has still its ancient power,
No word from Thee can fruitless fall;
Hear in this solemn evening hour,
And in Thy mercy heal us all.

Rev. Henry Twells. (1823—) 1868. ab.

SHINING SHORE. 8, 7. D. — George Frederick Root. (1820—) 18.6.

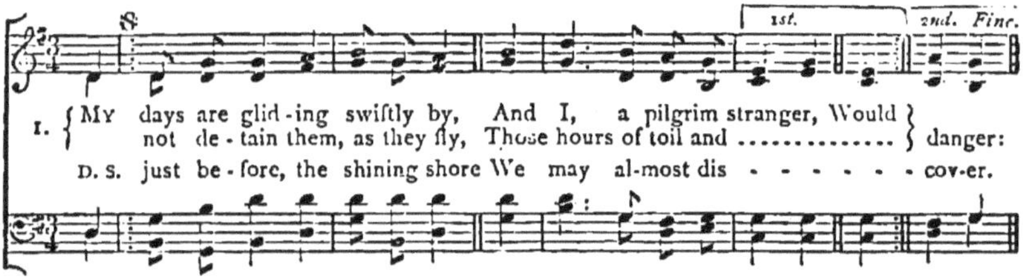
1st.
2nd. Fine.
1. { My days are glid - ing swiftly by, And I, a pilgrim stranger, Would }
{ not de - tain them, as they fly, Those hours of toil and .... } danger:
D. S. just be - fore, the shining shore We may al-most dis - - - - - - - cov-er.

Chorus.
D. S.
For, O we stand on Jordan's strand; Our friends are pass - ing ov - er; And

277 *Jordan's Strand.*

2 We'll gird our loins, my brethren dear,
Our heavenly home discerning;
Our absent Lord has left us word,
"Let every lamp be burning:" *Cho.*

3 Let sorrow's rudest tempest blow,
Each cord on earth to sever; [home,
Our King says, "Come!" and there's our
Forever, O forever: *Cho.*

Rev. David Nelson. (1793—1844.) 1835.

Work, for the Night is Coming. 7, 6, 7, 5. — Lowell Mason. (1792—1872.)

1. Work, for the night is com - ing, Work thro' the morning hours; Work while the dew is spark - ling,
D. S. Work, for the night is com - ing,

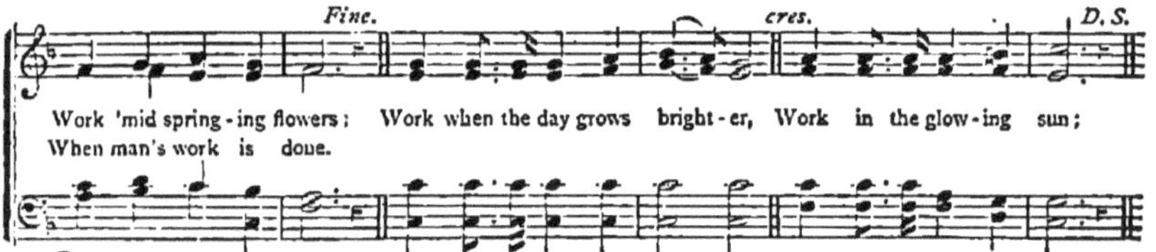
Fine.
cres.
D. S.
Work 'mid spring - ing flowers; Work when the day grows bright - er, Work in the glow - ing sun;
When man's work is done.

278 *Work.*

2 Work, for the night is coming,
Work through the sunny noon;
Fill brightest hours with labor,
Rest comes sure and soon.

Give every flying minute
Something to keep in store:
Work, for the night is coming,
When man works no more.

Rev. Sidney Dyer.

FREDERICK. 11. George Kingsley. (1811—) 1834.

1. I WOULD not live alway; I ask not to stay Where storm af - ter
storm ris - es dark o'er the way; The few lu - rid morn - ings, that
dawn on us here, Are enough for life's woes, full e - nough for its cheer.

279 *"I would not live alway."*

2 I would not live alway, thus fettered by sin,
Temptation without and corruption within,
E'en the rapture of pardon is mingled with fears,
And the cup of thanksgiving with penitent tears.

3 Who, who would live alway, away from his God?
Away from yon heaven, that blissful abode,
Where the rivers ot pleasure flow o'er the bright plains,
And the noontide of glory eternally reigns;

4 Where the saints of all ages in harmony meet,
Their Saviour and brethren transported to greet;
While the anthems of rapture unceasingly roll,
And the smile of the Lord is the feast of the soul.

Rev. William Augustus Muhlenberg. (1796—) 1823.

280 *Longing for Rest.*

Ps. lv.

1 O HAD I, my Saviour, the wings of a dove,
How soon would I soar to Thy presence above;
How soon would I flee where the weary have rest,
And hide all my cares in Thy sheltering breast.

2 I flutter, I struggle, I pant to get free;
I feel me a captive while banished from Thee:
A pilgrim and stranger, the desert I roam,
And look on to heaven, and long to be home.

3 Ah, there the wild tempest forever shall cease;
No billow shall ruffle that haven of peace
Temptation and trouble alike shall depart
All tears from the eye, and all sin from the heart.

Rev. Henry Francis Lyte. (1793--1847). 1834

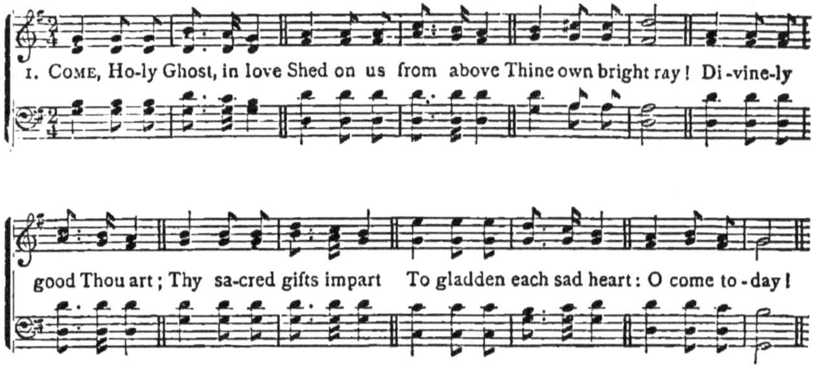
1. Come, Ho-ly Ghost, in love Shed on us from above Thine own bright ray! Di-vine-ly
good Thou art; Thy sa-cred gifts impart To gladden each sad heart: O come to-day!

281

"Veni, Sancte Spiritus."

2 Come, tenderest Friend, and best,
Our most delightful guest,
With soothing power:
Rest, which the weary know,
Shade, 'mid the noontide glow,
Peace, when deep griefs o'erflow,
Cheer us, this hour!

3 Come, Light serene, and still
Our inmost bosoms fill;
Dwell in each breast;
We know no dawn but Thine;
Send forth Thy beams divine,
On our dark souls to shine,
And make us blest!

4 Come, all the faithful bless;
Let all who Christ confess,
His praise employ:
Give virtue's rich reward;
Victorious death accord,
And, with our glorious Lord,
Eternal joy!

Robert II., King of France. (972—1031.)
Tr. by Rev Ray Palmer. (1808—) 1858.

282

Evening Prayer.

1 Father of love and power,
Guard Thou our evening hour
Shield with Thy might:
For all Thy care this day
Our grateful thanks we pay,
And to our Father pray,
Bless us to-night.

2 Jesus Immanuel,
Come in Thy love to dwell
In hearts contrite:
For many sins we grieve,
But we Thy grace receive,
And in Thy word believe;
Bless us to-night.

3 Spirit of truth and love,
Life-giving, holy Dove,
Shed forth Thy light:
Heal every sinner's smart,
Still every throbbing heart
And Thine own peace impart;
Bless us to-night.

George Rawson. (1807—) 1853.

ARLINGTON. C. M. Thomas Augustine Arne. (1710—1778.) 1744.

1. LIGHT of the lone - ly pil-grim's heart, Star of the com - ing day,
A - rise, and, with Thy morn-ing beams, Chase all our griefs a - way.

283 *Watching for the Morning.*

1 LIGHT of the lonely pilgrim's heart,
Star of the coming day,
Arise, and, with Thy morning beams,
Chase all our griefs away

2 Come, blessèd Lord, bid every shore
And answering island sing
The praises of Thy royal name,
And own Thee as their King.

3 Bid the whole earth, responsive now
To the bright world above,
Break forth in rapturous strains of joy
In memory of Thy love.

4 Lord, Lord, Thy fair creation groans,
The air, the earth, the sea,
In unison with all our hearts,
And calls aloud for Thee.

5 Thine was the cross, with all its fruits
Of grace and peace divine:
Be thine the crown of glory now,
The palm of victory Thine.

Sir Edward Denny. (1796—) 1839. ab.

284 *"Come, Lord Jesus."*
Rev. xxii. 20.

1 HOPE of our hearts, O Lord, appear:
Thou glorious Star of day,
Shine forth, and chase the dreary night,
With all our tears, away.

2 Strangers on earth, we wait for Thee;
O leave the Father's throne,
Come with a shout of victory, Lord,
And claim us as Thine own.

3 O bid the bright archangel, now,
The trump of God prepare,
To call Thy saints—the quick, the dead,
To meet Thee in the air.

4 No resting place we seek on earth,
No loveliness we see,
Our eye is on the royal crown,
Prepared for us and Thee.

5 There, near Thy heart, upon the throne
Thy ransomed Bride shall see
What grace was in the bleeding Lamb,
Who died to make her free.

Sir Edward Denny (1796—) 1839. ab.

THE OLD, OLD STORY. 7, 6. D.

William Howard Doane. (1832—) 1869.

1. Tell me the old, old sto - ry Of unseen things a - bove, Of Je - sus and His glo - ry, Of
D. S. For I am weak and wea - ry, And
Fine.
D. S.
Chorus.
Je - sus and His love. Tell me the sto - ry sim - ply, As to a lit - tle child, Tell me the old, old
help-less and de - filed.
sto - ry, Tell me the old, old sto - ry, Tell me the old, old sto - ry Of Je - sus and His love.

285

"Tell me the Old, Old Story."

2 Tell me the story slowly,
  That I may take it in—
That wonderful redemption,
  God's remedy for sin.
Tell me the story often,
  For I forget so soon!
The "early dew" of morning
  Has passed away at noon.

3 Tell me the story softly,
  With earnest tones, and grave;
Remember, I'm the sinner
  Whom Jesus came to save.
Tell me that story always,
  If you would really be,
In any time of trouble,
  A comforter to me.

4 Tell me the same old story,
  When you have cause to fear
That this world's empty glory
  Is costing me too dear.
Yes, and when that world's glory
  Is drawing on my soul,
Tell me the old, old story:
  "Christ Jesus makes thee whole."

Miss Kate Hankey. 1865.

286

The coming Millennium.

1 Awake, awake, O Zion,
  Put on Thy strength divine,
Thy garments bright in beauty,
  The bridal dress be Thine:
Jerusalem, the holy,
  To purity restored;
Meek Bride, all fair and lowly,
  Go forth to meet Thy Lord.

2 The Lamb who bore our sorrows
  Comes down to earth again;
No Sufferer now, but Victor,
  For evermore to reign;
To reign in every nation,
  To rule in every zone:
O wide-world coronation,
  In every heart a throne.

3 Awake, awake, O Zion,
  The bridal day draws nigh,
The day of signs and wonders,
  And marvels from on high,
Thy sun uprises slowly,
  But keep thou watch and ward;
Fair Bride, all pure and lowly,
  Go forth to meet thy Lord.

Benjamin Gough. (1805—) 1865. ab.

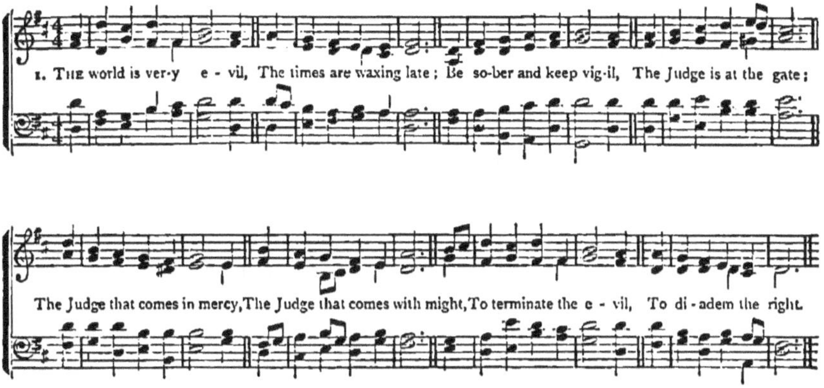
1. The world is ver-y e - vil, The times are waxing late; Be so-ber and keep vig-il, The Judge is at the gate;
The Judge that comes in mercy, The Judge that comes with might, To terminate the e - vil, To di - adem the right.

287 *"Hora novissima."*

2 Arise, arise, good Christian,
  Let right to wrong succeed;
Let penitential sorrow
  To heavenly gladness lead;
To light that hath no evening,
  That knows no moon, nor sun,
The light so new and golden,
  The light that is but one.

3 O Home of fadeless splendor,
  Of flowers that fear no thorn,
Where they shall dwell as children
  Who here as exiles mourn.
'Midst power that knows no limit,
  Where wisdom has no bound,
The beatific vision
  Shall glad the saints around.

Bernard of Cluny. c. 1145.
Tr. by Rev. John Mason Neale. (1818—1866.) 1858. ab. and sl. alt.

288 *"Ermuntert euch, ihr Frommen."*

1 REJOICE, rejoice, believers,
  And let your lights appear;
The evening is advancing,
  And darker night is near.
The Bridegroom is arising,
  And soon He will draw nigh;
Up, pray, and watch, and wrestle,
  At midnight comes the cry.

2 See that your lamps are burning,
  Replenish them with oil;
Look now for your salvation,
  The end of sin and toil.
The watchers on the mountain
  Proclaim the Bridegroom near,
Go meet Him as He cometh,
  With hallelujahs clear.

3 Our hope and expectation,
  O Jesus, now appear;
Arise, thou Sun so longed for,
  O'er this benighted sphere.
With hearts and hands uplifted,
  We plead, O Lord, to see
The day of earth's redemption,
  And ever be with Thee.

Laurentius Laurenti. (1660—1722.)
Tr. by Miss Jane Borthwick. 1853. ab. and sl. alt.

TELL THE STORY. 7, 6. D. 122 William Gustavus Fischer. (1835—) 1869.

1. I LOVE to tell the sto-ry, Of un-seen things above, Of Je-sus and His glory, Of Je-sus and His love.
I love to tell the sto-ry, Be-cause I know 'tis true; It sat-is-fies my longings, As nothing else can do.
CHORUS.
I love to tell the sto-ry, 'Twill be my theme in glory, To tell the old, old sto-ry Of Jesus and His love.

289 "*I love to tell the Story.*"

2 I love to tell the story;
More wonderful it seems,
Than all the golden fancies
Of all our golden dreams.
I love to tell the story,
It did so much for me!
And that is just the reason
I tell it now to thee.

3 I love to tell the story;
'Tis pleasant to repeat,
What seems, each time I tell it,
More wonderfully sweet.
I love to tell the story,
For some have never heard
The message of salvation,
From God's own holy word.

4 I love to tell the story;
For those who know it best,
Seem hungering and thirsting
To hear it like the rest.
And when, in scenes of glory,
I sing the New, New Song,
'Twill be the Old, Old Story
That I have loved so long.

Miss Kate Hankey. 1865.

290 "*The Lord's Salvation.*"

1 O THAT the Lord's salvation
Were out of Zion come,
To heal His ancient nation,
To lead His outcasts home.
How long the holy City
Shall heathen feet profane?
Return, O Lord, in pity;
Rebuild her walls again.

2 Let fall Thy rod of terror,
Thy saving grace impart;
Roll back the veil of error,
Release the fettered heart.
Let Israel, home returning
Her lost Messiah see;
Give oil of joy for mourning,
And bind Thy Church to Thee.

Rev. Henry Francis Lyte. (1793—1847.) 18—

EWING. 7, 6. D. Bp. Alexander Ewing. (- 1873.) 1861.

1 JE-RU-SA-LEM the glor-ious, The home of the elect, O dear and future vision That eager hearts ex-pect;
E'en now by faith I see thee, E'en here thy walls discern; To thee my thoughts are kindled, And strive and pant and yearn.

291

"Urbs Syon inclyta, Gloria."

1 JERUSALEM the glorious,
The home of the elect,
O dear and future vision
That eager hearts expect:
E'en now by faith I see thee,
E'en here thy walls discern;
To thee my thoughts are kindled,
And strive and pant and yearn.

2 New mansion of new people,
Whom God's own love and light
Promote, increase, make holy,
Identify, unite.
And there the band of prophets
United praise ascribes,
And there the twelve-fold chorus
Of Israel's ransomed tribes.

3 And there the Sole-Begotten
Is Lord in regal state;
He Judah's mystic Lion,
He, Lamb immaculate.
O fields that know no sorrow,
O state that fears no strife,
O princely bowers, O land of flowers,
O realm and home of life.

Bernard of Cluny. c. 1145.
Tr. by Rev. John Mason Neale. 1851. alt.

292

"Urbs Syon aurea.

1 JERUSALEM the golden,
With milk and honey blest,
Beneath thy contemplation
Sink heart and voice oppresst:
I know not, O I know not
What social joys are there;
What radiancy of glory,
What light beyond compare.

2 They stand, those halls of Zion,
All jubilant with song,
And bright with many an angel,
And all the martyr throng:
The Prince is ever in them,
The daylight is serene;
The pastures of the blessèd
Are decked in glorious sheen.

3 There is the throne of David;
And there, from care released,
The shout of them that triumph,
The song of them that feast;
And they who, with their leader,
Have conquered in the fight,
Forever and forever
Are clad in robes of white.

Bernard of Cluny. c. 1145.
Tr. by Rev. John Mason Neale. 1851. alt.

ALFORD. 7, 6, 8, 6. Rev. John Bacchus Dykes.

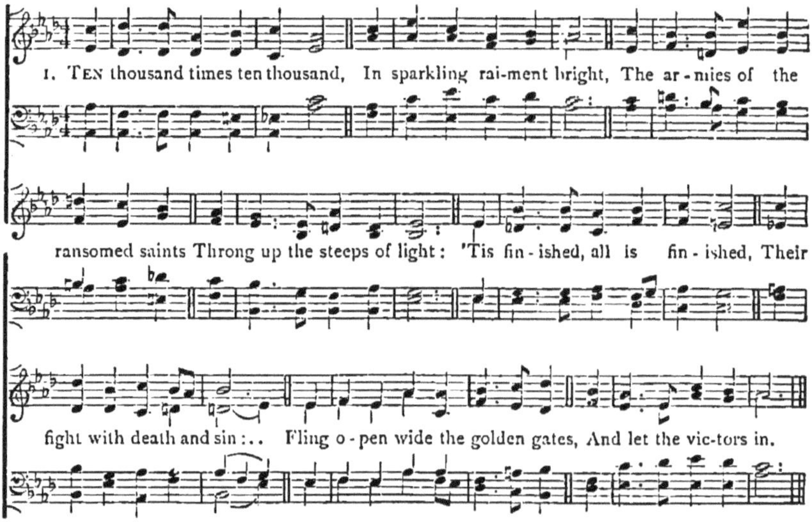
1. TEN thousand times ten thousand, In sparkling rai-ment bright, The ar-mies of the
ransomed saints Throng up the steeps of light: 'Tis fin-ished, all is fin-ished, Their
fight with death and sin:.. Fling o-pen wide the golden gates, And let the vic-tors in.

293 *The Saints marching up.*

2 What rush of hallelujahs
Fills all the earth and sky;
What ringing of a thousand harps
Bespeaks the triumph nigh.
O day, for which Creation
And all its tribes were made;
O joy, for all its former woes
A thousand-fold repaid.

3 O then what raptured greetings
On Canaan's happy shore;
What knitting severed friendships up,
Where partings are no more.
Then eyes with joy shall sparkle,
That brimmed with tears of late:
Orphans no longer fatherless,
Nor widows desolate.

Rev. Henry Alford. (1810—1871.) 1866.

294 *Delighting in God's Day.*

1 THY holy day's returning
Our hearts exult to see;
And with devotion burning,
Ascend, O God, to Thee.
To-day with purest pleasure,
Our thoughts from earth withdraw;
We search for heavenly treasure,
We learn Thy holy law.

2 We join to sing Thy praises,
Lord of the Sabbath day;
Each voice in gladness raises
Its loudest, sweetest lay.
Thy richest mercies sharing,
Inspire us with Thy love,
By grace our souls preparing
For nobler praise above.

Rev. Ray Palmer. (1808—) 1834.

BEULAH. 7. D. 125 Irish Melody. Arr. by Elam Ives, Jr. (1802—1864.) 1846.

1. Palms of glo - ry, raiment bright, Crowns that never fade a - way, Gird and deck the saints in light,
D. S. And proclaim, in joy - ful psalms,
Fine.
D. S.
Priests, and kings, and conquerors they. Yet the conquerors bring their palms To the Lamb a - midst the throne,
Vic - tory through His cross a - lone.

295

Heaven in Prospect.
Rev. vii. 9.

2 Kings for harps their crowns resign,
Crying, as they strike the chords,
"Take the kingdom, it is Thine,
King of kings, and Lord of lords."
Round the altar, priests confess,
If their robes are white as snow,
'Twas the Saviour's righteousness,
And His blood, that made them so.

3 Who were these?—On earth they dwelt,
Sinners once of Adam's race,
Guilt and fear, and suffering felt,
But were saved by sovereign grace.
They were mortal, too, like us:
Ah, when we, like them, shall die,
May our souls, translated thus,
Triumph, reign, and shine on high.

James Montgomery. (1771—1854.) 1829.

296

The Song of the Sealed.
Rev. vii. 9—16.

WHAT are these in bright array,
This innumerable throng,
Round the altar night and day,
Hymning one triumphant song:
"Worthy is the Lamb, once slain,
Blessing, honor, glory, power,
Wisdom, riches, to obtain,
New dominion every hour."

2 These through fiery trials trod;
These from great afflictions came;
Now, before the throne of God,
Sealed with His Almighty Name;
Clad in raiment pure and white,
Victor-palms in every hand,
Through their dear Redeemer's might,
More than conquerors they stand.

3 Hunger, thirst, disease unknown,
On immortal fruits they feed;
Them the Lamb amidst the throne,
Shall to living fountains lead;
Joy and gladness banish sighs,
Perfect love dispels all fear,
And forever from their eyes
God shall wipe away the tear.

James Montgomery. 1819, 1853.

GREENWOOD. S. M. 126 Joseph E. Sweetser. (1825—) 1849

1 The Church has wait - ed long Her ab - sent Lord to see;
And still in lone - li - ness she waits, A friend-less stran-ger she.

297 *Advent.*

1 THE Church has waited long
  Her absent Lord to see;
And still in loneliness she waits,
  A friendless stranger she.

2 Age after age has gone,
  Sun after sun has set,
And still, in weeds of widowhood,
  She weeps a mourner yet.

3 Saint after saint on earth
  Has lived, and loved, and died;
And as they left us one by one,
  We laid them side by side;

4 We laid them down to sleep,
  But not in hope forlorn;
We laid them but to ripen there
  Till the last glorious morn.

5 The whole creation groans,
  And waits to hear that voice
That shall restore her comeliness,
  And make her wastes rejoice.

6 Come, Lord, and wipe away
  The curse, the sin, the stain,
And make this blighted world of ours
  Thine own fair world again.

Rev. Horatius Bonar. (1808—) 1857. ab.

298 *"Come, Lord."*

1 COME, Lord, and tarry not:
  Bring the long-looked-for day,
O why these years of waiting here,
  These ages of delay?

2 Come, for creation groans,
  Impatient of Thy stay,
Worn out with these long years of ill,
  These ages of delay.

3 Come, for the corn is ripe,
  Put in Thy sickle now;
Reap the great harvest of the earth,
  Sower and Reaper, Thou.

4 Come in Thy glorious might,
  Come with the iron rod,
Scattering Thy foes before Thy face,
  Most mighty Son of God.

5 Come, and make all things new;
  Build up this ruined earth;
Restore our faded Paradise,
  Creation's second birth.

6 Come, and begin Thy reign
  Of everlasting peace;
Come, take the kingdom to Thyself,
  Great King of righteousness.

Rev. Horatius Bonar. 1857. ab.

REVIVE US AGAIN. 11, 12. English Melody.

1. We praise Thee, O God, for the Son of Thy love, For Je-sus who died, and is now gone a-bove. Hal-le-
CHORUS.
lu-jah! Thine the glory, Hal-le-lu-jah! A-men. Hal-le-lu-jah! Thine the glory, Re-vive us a-gain.

299

2 We praise Thee, O God, for Thy Spirit of Light,
Who has shown us our Saviour, and scattered our night.

3 All glory and praise to the Lamb that was slain,
Who has borne all our sins, and has cleansed every stain.

4 All glory and praise to the God of all grace,
Who has bought us, and sought us, and guided our ways.

5 Revive us again; fill each heart with Thy love;
May each soul be rekindled with fire from above.

Rev. W. P. Mackay. 1863.

SOLID ROCK. L. M. 6 l. William Batchelder Bradbury. (1816—1868.) 1865.

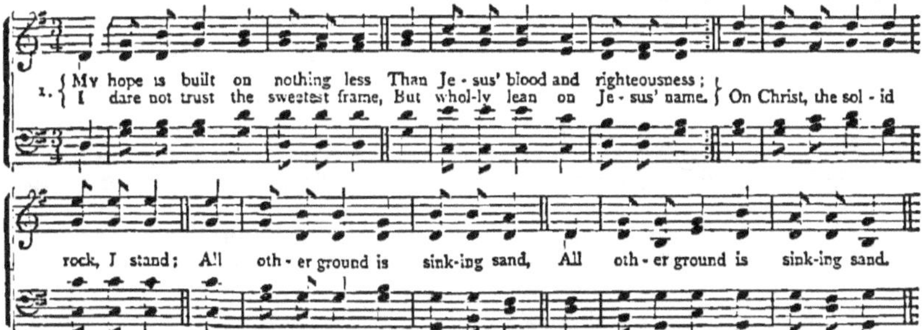
1. { My hope is built on nothing less Than Je-sus' blood and righteousness; / I dare not trust the sweetest frame, But whol-ly lean on Je-sus' name. } On Christ, the sol-id
rock, I stand; All oth-er ground is sink-ing sand, All oth-er ground is sink-ing sand.

300

The solid Rock.

2 When darkness seems to veil His face,
I rest on His unchanging grace;
In every high and stormy gale,
My anchor holds within the veil:
On Christ, the solid rock, I stand;
All other ground is sinking sand.

3 His oath, His covenant, and blood,
Support me in the whelming flood:
When all around my soul gives way,
He then is all my hope and stay:
On Christ, the solid rock, I stand;
All other ground is sinking sand.

Rev Edward Mote. 1863.

PARADISE. P. M. Rev. John Bacchus Dykes. 1861.

mf
p
cres.
1. O PAR-ADISE, O Par-a-dise, Who doth not crave for rest, Who would not seek the
p
CHORUS.
happy land Where they that loved are blest? Where loyal hearts and true Stand ev-er in the
cres.
dim.
rall.
light, All rapture through and through, In God's most ho-ly sight.

301 *Paradise.*

2 O Paradise, O Paradise,
The world is growing old;
Who would not be at rest and free
Where love is never cold? *Cho.*

3 O Paradise, O Paradise,
I want to sin no more,
I want to be as pure on earth
As on Thy spotless shore; *Cho.*

O PARADISE. 8, 6, 8, 6; 6, 6, 6, 6. J. BARNBY, 1866.

A-men.

NEW JERUSALEM. 7, 6, 7, 7, 7. — Old English Melody.

1. We are on our jour-ney home, Where Christ our Lord is gone; We shall meet a-round His throne,
When He makes His peo-ple one In the new, In the new Je - ru - sa - lem.
In the new Je - ru - sa - lem.

302 *"New Jerusalem."*

2 We can see that distant home,
Though clouds rise dark between:
Faith views the radiant dome,
And a lustre flashes keen
‖:From the new:‖ Jerusalem.

3 O glory shining far
From the never-setting Sun,
O trembling morning-star,
Our journey's almost done
‖:To the new:‖ Jerusalem.

SWEET STORY. 11, 8, 12, 9. — English.

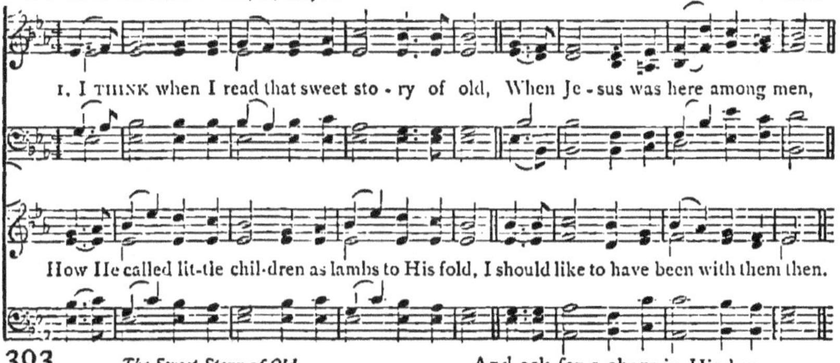
1. I THINK when I read that sweet sto - ry of old, When Je - sus was here among men,
How He called lit-tle chil-dren as lambs to His fold, I should like to have been with them then.

303 *The Sweet Story of Old.*

2 I wish that His hands had been placed on my head,
That His arms had been thrown around me,
And that I might have seen His kind look when He said,
"Let the little ones come unto Me."

3 Yet still to His footstool in prayer I may go,
And ask for a share in His love;
And if I thus earnestly seek Him below,
I shall see Him and hear Him above.

4 In that beautiful place He has gone to prepare
For all who are washed and forgiven;
And many dear children shall be with Him there,
"For of such is the kingdom of heaven."

Mrs. Jemima Luke. 1841.

WE SHALL MEET. 8, 6, 7, 7, 7, 6. 130 Hubert Platt Main. (1833—) 1867.

1. We shall meet be-yond the riv - er, By - and - by, by - and - by; And the dark - ness
shall be o - ver, By - and - by, by - and - by; With the toil - some jour-ney done, And the
glo-rious bat - tle won, We shall shine forth as the sun, By - and - by, by - and - by.

304

"We shall meet."

2 We shall strike the harps of glory,
By-and-by, by-and-by;
We shall sing redemption's story,
By-and-by, by-and-by;
And the strains forevermore
Shall resound in sweetness o'er
Yonder everlasting shore,
By-and-by, by-and-by.

3 We shall see and be like Jesus,
By-and-by, by-and-by;
Who a crown of life will give us,
By-and-by, by-and-by:
And the angels who fulfill
All the mandates of His will,
Shall attend and love us still,
By-and-by, by-and-by.

4 There our tears shall all cease flowing,
By-and-by, by-and-by;
And with sweetest rapture knowing,
By-and-by, by-and-by;
All the blest ones who have gone
To the land of light and song,
We with shoutings shall rejoin,
By-and-by, by-and-by.

Rev. John Atkinson. 1867.

305

1 Glory be to the Father, and to the Son;
And to the Holy Ghost;
As it was in the beginning, is now, and ever shall be:
World without end. Amen.

DIX. 7.61. From the German Arr. by William Henry Monk 1861.

1. { God of mer - cy, God of grace, Show the brightness of Thy face; }
{ Shine up - on us, Sav - iour, shine, Fill Thy Church with light di - vine; }
And Thy sav - ing health ex - tend Un - to earth's re - mot - est end.

306 *Prayer for Light and Enlargement.*

Ps. lxvii.

2 Let the people praise Thee, Lord,
Be by all that live adored:
Let the nations shout and sing,
Glory to their Saviour-King;
At Thy feet their tributes pay,
And Thy holy will obey.

3 Let the people praise Thee, Lord,
Earth shall then her fruits afford:
God to man His blessing give,
Man to God devoted live;
All below, and all above,
One in joy, and light, and love.

Rev. Henry Francis Lyte. (1793—1847.) 1834.

307 *Morning Hymn.*

1 CHRIST, whose glory fills the skies,
Christ, the true, the only Light,
Sun of righteousness, arise,
Triumph o'er the shades of night:
Dayspring from on high, be near;
Daystar, in my heart appear.

2 Dark and cheerless is the morn,
Unaccompanied by Thee;
Joyless is the day's return,
Till Thy mercy's beams I see:
Till they inward light impart,
Glad my eyes, and warm my heart.

3 Visit then this soul of mine,
Pierce the gloom of sin and grief;
Fill me, Radiancy divine,
Scatter all my unbelief:
More and more Thyself display,
Shining to the perfect day.

Rev. Charles Wesley. (1708—1788.) 174

308 *Cause Thy Face to shine.*

Ps. lxvii.

1 ON Thy Church, O Power divine,
Cause Thy glorious face to shine;
Till the nations, from afar,
Hail her as their guiding star;
Till her sons, from zone to zone,
Make Thy great salvation known.

2 Then shall God, with lavish hand,
Scatter blessings o'er the land;
Earth shall yield her rich increase,
Every breeze shall whisper peace,
And the world's remotest bound
With the voice of praise resound.

Miss Harriet Auber. (1773—1862.) 1829.

WAVE. 8, 7, 4. Arr. by William Batchelder Bradbury. (1816—1868.) 1844.

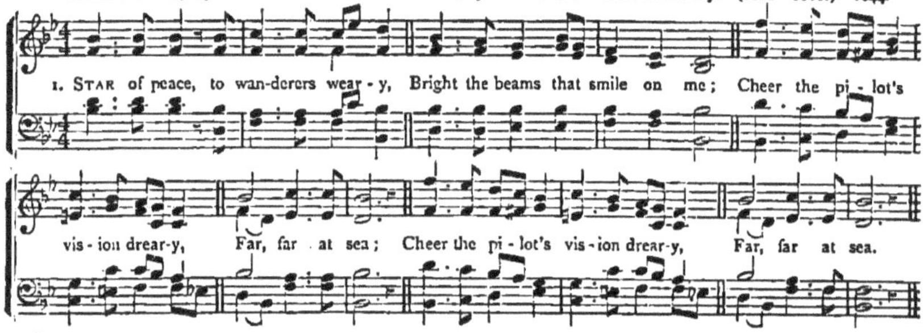
1. Star of peace, to wan-derers wear-y, Bright the beams that smile on me; Cheer the pi-lot's
vis-ion drear-y, Far, far at sea; Cheer the pi-lot's vis-ion drear-y, Far, far at sea.

309 *The guiding Star.*

2 Star of hope, gleam on the billow,
Bless the soul that sighs for thee;
Bless the sailor's lonely pillow,
Far, far at sea.

3 Star of faith, when winds are mocking
All his toil, he flies to thee;
Save him on the billows rocking,
Far, far at sea.

4 Star divine, O safely guide him,
Bring the wanderer home to thee:
Sore temptations long have tried him,
Far, far at sea.

Mrs. Jane Bell Cross Simpson. 1830. ab.

THE LORD WILL PROVIDE. 11, 6, 5. Calvin Sears Harrington. c. 1864.

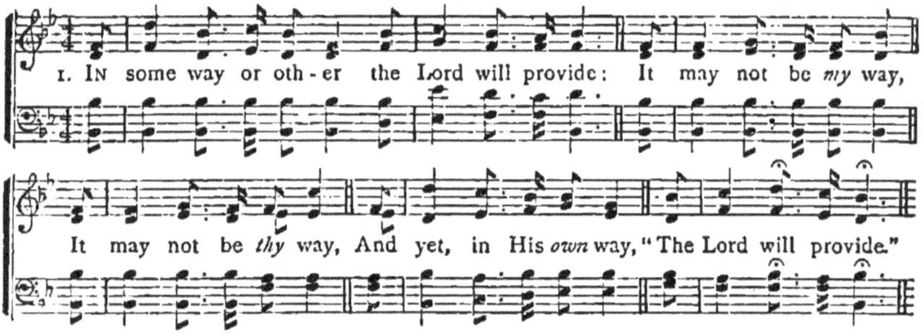
1. In some way or oth-er the Lord will provide: It may not be *my* way,
It may not be *thy* way, And yet, in His *own* way, "The Lord will provide."

310 *"The Lord will provide."*

2 At some time or other the Lord will provide:
It may not be *my* time,
It may not be *thy* time,
And yet, in His *own* time,
"The Lord will provide."

3 Despond then no longer; the Lord will provide:
And this be the token,
No word He hath spoken
Was ever yet broken;
"The Lord will provide."

4 March on, then, right boldly, the sea shall divide:
The pathway made glorious,
With shoutings victorious,
We'll join in the chorus,
"The Lord will provide."

Mrs. Mary Ann Woodbridge Cooke. (1 07-1874.) c. 1864.

MAGDALENE. 6, 5. Rev. John Bacchus Dykes. 1861.

1. In the hour of tri - al, Je - sus, pray for me; Lest by base de - ni - al I de-part from Thee:
When Thou seest me wav-er, With a look re - call, Nor for fear or fa - vor, Suf- fer me to fall.

311 *The Hour of Trial.*

2 If with sore affliction
  Thou in love chastise,
Pour Thy benediction
  On the sacrifice:
Then, upon Thine altar
  Freely offered up,
Though the flesh may falter,
  Faith shall drain the cup.

3 When in dust and ashes
  To the grave I sink,
While heaven's glory flashes
  O'er the shelving brink,
On Thy truth relying
  Through that mortal strife,
Lord, receive me, dying,
  To eternal life.

James Montgomery. (1771—1854.) 1853. ab.

312 *House set in Order.*

1 Set thy house in order,
  Thou shalt die, not live;
May the voice to each one
  Solemn warning give:
Pilgrims here and strangers,
  Weak and frail alike,
Who can tell among us
  Where the blow may strike?

2 Set thy house in order,
  All its bulwarks tell;
Try the ground beneath thee,
  Stir and delve it well:
Soon shall break the tempest;
  Wouldst thou bide the shock?
Hearer be and doer,
  Founded on the rock.

3 Set thy house in order,
  Gather up thy stores,
Every weapon brighten
  For thy Captain's wars
Sort out all thy treasures,
  Earthly dross remove;
Three alone are lasting,
  Faith, and hope, and love.

Rev. Henry Alford. (1810—1871.) 1865. ab.

AURELIA. 7, 6. D. Samuel Sebastian Wesley. 1868.

1. I NEED Thee, pre-cious Je-sus, For I am full of sin; My soul is dark and
guilt-y, My heart is dead with-in; I need the cleans-ing fount-ain Where
I can al-ways flee, The blood of Christ most pre-cious, The sin-ner's per-fect plea.

313

"He is precious."
1 Pet. ii. 7.

2 I need Thee, precious Jesus,
For I am very poor;
A stranger and a pilgrim,
I have no earthly store;
I need the love of Jesus
To cheer me on my way,
To guide my doubting footsteps,
To be my strength and stay.

3 I need Thee, precious Jesus,
I need a friend like Thee,
A friend to soothe and pity,
A friend to care for me.
I need the heart of Jesus
To feel each anxious care,
To tell my every trouble,
And all my sorrows share.

4 I need Thee, precious Jesus,
And hope to see Thee soon,
Encircled with the rainbow,
And seated on Thy throne:
There, with Thy blood-bought children,
My joy shall ever be,
To sing Thy praises, Jesus,
To gaze, my Lord, on Thee.

Rev. Frederick Whitfield. (1829—.) 1859. ab. and sl. alt.

314

"Still keep me."

1 O LAMB of God, still keep me
Near to Thy wounded side;
'Tis only there in safety
And peace I can abide.
What foes and snares surround me,
What doubts and fears within!
The grace that sought and found me,
Alone can keep me clean.

2 Soon shall my eyes behold Thee
With rapture face to face;
One-half hath not been told me
Of all Thy power and grace;
Thy beauty, Lord, and glory,
The wonders of Thy love,
Shall be the endless story
Of all Thy saints above.

James George Deck. 1857. ab.

CRUCIFIX. 7, 6. D. — Greek Melody.

1. In heaven-ly love a-biding, No change my heart shall fear;
And safe in such con-fid-ing, For noth-ing changes here.
The storm may roar with-out me,
My heart may low be laid,
But God is round a-bout me,
And can I be dis-mayed?

315

"I will fear no Evil."
Ps. xxiii. 4.

1 In heavenly love abiding,
No change my heart shall fear;
And safe is such confiding,
For nothing changes here.
The storm may roar without me,
My heart may low be laid,
But God is round about me,
And can I be dismayed?

2 Wherever He may guide me,
No want shall turn me back;
My Shepherd is beside me,
And nothing can I lack.
His wisdom ever waketh,
His sight is never dim,
He knows the way He taketh,
And I will walk with Him.

3 Green pastures are before me,
Which yet I have not seen;
Bright skies will soon be o'er me,
Where darkest clouds have been.
My hope I can not measure,
My path to life is free,
My Saviour has my treasure,
And He will walk with me.

Miss Anna Laetitia Waring. 1850. sl. alt.

316

"I lay my sins on Jesus."

1 I LAY my sins on Jesus,
The spotless Lamb of God;
He bears them all and frees us
From the accursèd load.
I bring my guilt to Jesus,
To wash my crimson stains
White in His blood most precious,
Till not a spot remains.

2 I lay my wants on Jesus,
All fullness dwells in Him;
He healeth my diseases,
He doth my soul redeem.
I lay my griefs on Jesus,
My burdens and my cares;
He from them all releases,
He all my sorrows shares.

3 I rest my soul on Jesus,
This weary soul of mine;
His right hand me embraces,
I on his breast recline.
I love the name of Jesus,
Immanuel, Christ, the Lord;
Like fragrance on the breezes,
His name abroad is poured.

4 I long to be like Jesus,
Meek, loving, lowly, mild;
I long to be like Jesus,
The Father's Holy Child;
I long to be with Jesus,
Amid the heavenly throng;
To sing with saints His praises,
To learn the angels' song.

H. Bonar. 18[illegible]

SALVATION. 7, 6. Johann C. W. A. Mozart (1756–1791.)

1. When, His sal-va - tion bringing, To Zi - on Je - sus came, The children all stood
sing - ing Ho - san - na to His name. Nor did their zeal of - fend Him, But
as He rode a - long, He let them still at - tend Him, And smiled to hear their song.

317 *The Children in the Temple.*
Matt. xxi. 15, 16.

2 And since the Lord retaineth
His love to children still,
Though now as King He reigneth
On Zion's heavenly hill;
We'll flock around His banner,
We'll bow before His throne,
And cry aloud, Hosanna
To David's royal Son.

3 For should we fail proclaiming
Our great Redeemer's praise,
The stones, our silence shaming,
Would their hosannas raise.
But shall we only render
The tribute of our words?
No; while our hearts are tender,
They, too, shall be the Lord's.

Rev. Joshua King. 1830.

318 *"Shew forth His Salvation."*
Ps. xcvi. 2.

1 To Thee, my God and Saviour,
My heart exulting sings,
Rejoicing in Thy favor,
Almighty King of kings;
I'll celebrate Thy glory,
With all Thy saints above,
And tell the joyful story,
Of Thy redeeming love.

2 Soon as the morn with roses
Bedecks the dewy east,
And when the sun reposes
Upon the ocean's breast,
My voice in supplication,
Well pleased, Thou shalt hear:
O grant me Thy salvation,
And to my soul draw near.

3 By Thee through life supported,
I pass the dangerous road,
With heavenly hosts escorted
Up to their bright abode;
There cast my crown before Thee;
Now all my conflicts o'er,
And day and night adore Thee:
What can an angel more?

Rev. Thomas Haweis. (1732–1820.) 1792

VOX ANGELICA. *11, 10.* 137 Rev. John Bacchus Dykes. 1861.

1. HARK, hark, my soul : an - gel - ic songs are swell-ing O'er earth's green fields and ocean's wave-beat shore ;
How sweet the truth those blessèd strains are tell - ing Of that new life when sin shall be no more
CHORUS.
An - gels of Je - sus, An - gels of light, Sing - ing to wel - come the pil-grims of the night.

319

"*Pilgrims of the Night.*"

2 Onward we go, for still we hear them singing,
"Come, weary souls, for Jesus bids you come ;"
And through the dark, its echoes sweetly ringing,
The music of the Gospel leads us home. *Cho.*

3 Far, far away, like bells at evening pealing,
The voice of Jesus sounds o'er land and sea ;
And laden souls, by thousands meekly stealing,
Kind Shepherd, turn their weary steps to Thee. *Cho.*

4 Rest comes at length ; though life be long and dreary,
The day must dawn, and darksome night be past ;
Life's journey ends in welcome to the weary,
And heaven, the heart's true home, will come at last. *Cho.*

5 Angels, sing on : your faithful watches keeping,
Sing us sweet fragments of the songs above ;
Till morning's joy shall end the night of weeping,
And life's long shadows break in cloudless love. *Cho.*

Rev. Frederick William Faber. (1814—1863.) 1849. ab. and alt.

HALLE. 7. 6 l. From Francis Joseph Haydn. (1732—1809.) 1798.

1. { FA-THER, by Thy love and power, Comes a - gain the eve - ning hour;
Light has van-ished, la - bors cease, Wea - ry crea-tures rest in peace: }

We to Thee our-selves re - sign, Let our lat - est thoughts be Thine.

320

Evening Hymn.

2 Saviour, to Thy Father bear
This our feeble evening prayer;
Thou hast seen how oft to-day
We, like sheep, have gone astray;
Blessèd Saviour, we, through Thee,
Pray that we may pardoned be.

3 Holy Spirit, Breath of balm,
Fall on us in evening's calm;
Yet awhile, before we sleep,
We with Thee will vigil keep.
Melt our spirits, mould our will,
Soften, strengthen, comfort still.

4 Blessèd Trinity, be near
Through the hours of darkness drear;
Father, Son, and Holy Ghost,
Round us set th' angelic host,
Till the flood of morning rays
Wake us to a song of praise.

Prof. Joseph Anstice. (1808—1836.) 1836. ab. and alt.

321

Evening Hymn.

1 NOW from labor and from care
Evening hours have set me free,
In the work of praise and prayer,
Lord, I would converse with Thee;
O behold me from above,
Fill me with a Saviour's love.

2 Sin and sorrow, guilt and woe
Wither all my earthly joys;
Naught can charm me here below
But my Saviour's melting voice;
Lord, forgive, Thy grace restore,
Make me Thine forevermore.

5 For the blessings of this day,
For the mercies of this hour,
For the Gospel's cheering ray,
For the Spirit's quickening power,
Grateful notes to Thee I raise;
O accept the song of praise.

Thomas Hastings. (1784—1872.) 1832

EVENING HYMN. L. M. Thomas Tallis. (—1585.) c. 1567.

1. A-WAKE, my soul, and with the... sun Thy dai-ly stage of du-ty run;
Shake off dull sloth, and joy-ful rise To pay thy morn-ing sac-ri-fice.

322

A Morning Hymn.

2 Wake, and lift up thyself, my heart,
And with the angels bear thy part,
Who, all night long, unwearied sing
High praise to the eternal King.

3 All praise to Thee who safe hast kept,
And hast refreshed me whilst I slept;
Grant, Lord, when I from death shall wake,
I may of endless life partake.

4 Lord, I my vows to Thee renew;
Disperse my sins as morning dew;
Guide my first springs of thought and will,
And with Thyself my spirit fill.

5 Direct, control, suggest this day,
All I design, or do, or say;
That all my powers, with all their might,
In Thy sole glory may unite.

Bp. Thomas Ken. (1637—1711.) 1697, 1709. ab.

323

An Evening Hymn.

1 ALL praise to Thee, my God, this night,
For all the blessings of the light:
Keep me, O keep me, King of kings,
Beneath Thine own almighty wings.

2 Forgive me, Lord, for Thy dear Son,
The ill that I this day have done;
That with the world, myself, and Thee,
I, ere I sleep, at peace may be.

3 Teach me to live, that I may dread
The grave as little as my bed;
To die, that this vile body may
Rise glorious at the awful day.

4 O may my soul on Thee repose,
And may sweet sleep my eyelids close;
Sleep, that shall me more vigorous make,
To serve my God when I awake.

5 When in the night I sleepless lie,
My soul with heavenly thoughts supply,
Let no ill dreams disturb my rest,
No powers of darkness me molest.

6 Praise God, from whom all blessings flow
Praise Him, all creatures here below;
Praise Him above, ye heavenly host;
Praise Father, Son, and Holy Ghost.

Bp. Thomas Ken. 1697, 1709. ab.

PALMER. 11,5. Felix Mendelssohn-Bartholdy. (1809—1847.)

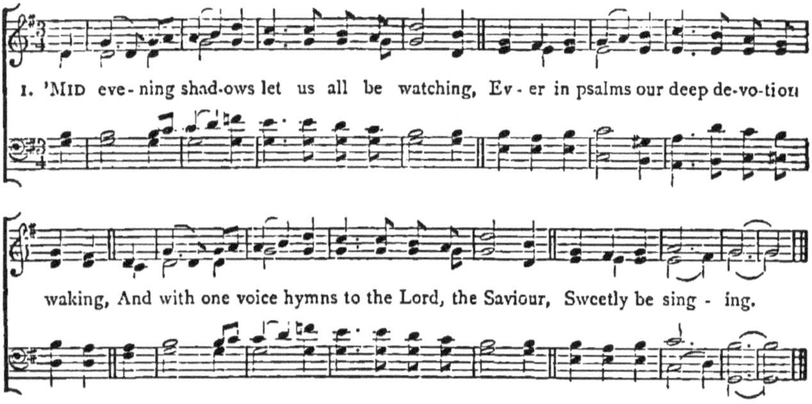
1. 'Mid eve-ning shad-ows let us all be watching, Ev-er in psalms our deep de-vo-tion
waking, And with one voice hymns to the Lord, the Saviour, Sweetly be sing - ing.

324 *An Evening Hymn.*

2 That to the Holy King our songs ascending,
We worthily, with all His saints, may enter
The heavenly temple, joyfully partaking
Life everlasting.

325 *A Morning Hymn.*

1 Behold, the shade of night is now receding,
Kindling with splendors fair the dawn is glowing,
With fervent hearts, O let us all implore Him,
Ruler Almighty:

2 That He, our God, will look on us in pity,
Send strength for weakness, grant us His salvation,

3 This grace O grant us, Godhead ever-blessèd,
Of Father, Son, and Holy Ghost in union,
Whose praises be through earth's most distant regions
Ever resounding.

Gregory. Tr. by Rev. Ray Palmer. 1871.

And with a Father's pure affection give us
Glory eternal.

3 This grace, O grant us, Godhead ever-blessèd,
Of Father, Son, and Holy Ghost in union,
Whose praises be through earth's most distant regions
Ever resounding.

Gregory. (540—604.)
Tr. by Rev. Ray Palmer. (1808—). 1871.

BERA. L. M. John Edgar Gould. (1822—) 1849

1. A LIT-TLE child the Sav - iour came, The mighty God was still His Name,
And an-gels worshipped, as He lay, The seeming in - fant of a day.

326 *"Let little Children come to Me."*

2 He who, a little child, began
The life divine to show to man,
Proclaims from heaven the message free,
"Let little children come to Me."

3 O give Thine angels charge, good Lord,
Them safely in Thy way to guard;
Thy blessing on their lives command,
And write their names upon Thy hand.

Rev. William Robertson. (—1743.) 1751. ab.

327 *Prayer for the Children of the Church.*

1 DEAR Saviour, if these lambs should stray
From Thy secure enclosure's bound,
And, lured by worldly joys away,
Among the thoughtless crowd be found;

2 Remember still that they are Thine,
That Thy dear sacred name they bear;
Think that the seal of love divine,
The sign of covenant grace, they wear.

3 In all their erring, sinful years,
O let them ne'er forgotten be;
Remember all the prayers and tears
Which made them consecrate to Thee.

4 And when these lips no more can pray,
These eyes can weep for them no more,
Turn Thou their feet from folly's way,
The wanderers to Thy fold restore.

Mrs. Ann Bradley Hyde. (—1872.) 1824.

328 *"Entirely Thine."*

1 LORD, I am Thine, entirely Thine,
Purchased and saved by blood divine;
With full consent Thine I would be,
And own Thy sovereign right in me.

2 Grant one poor sinner more a place,
Among the children of Thy grace;
A wretched sinner, lost to God,
But ransomed by Immanuel's blood.

3 Thine would I live, Thine would I die,
Be Thine through all eternity;
The vow is past beyond repeal;
Now will I set the solemn seal.

4 Here, at that cross where flows the
blood,
That bought my guilty soul for God,
Thee my new master now I call,
And consecrate to Thee my all.

5 Do Thou assist a feeble worm
The great engagement to perform;
Thy grace can full assistance lend,
And on that grace I dare depend.

Rev. Samuel Davies. (1724—1761.) 1769.

AVISON. 11, 11, 12, 11. Charles Avison. (1710—1770.)

SHOUT the glad tidings, ex - ult - ing - ly sing,..... Je - ru - sa - lem triumphs, Mes-
1st & 2d verses.
Ending for 3d verse.
si - ah is King! si - ah is King, Mes-si - ah is King, Mes-si - ah is King!
Fine.
1. Zi - on the mar - vel - ous sto - ry be tell - ing, The Son of the
high - est, how low - ly His birth, The bright - est arch - an - gel in
glo - ry ex - cel - ling, He stoops to re - deem thee, He reigns up - on earth.
D. C.

329

The City of God.

2 Tell how He cometh ; from nation to nation,
The heart-cheering news, let the earth echo round ;
How free to the faithful He offers salvation,
How His people with joy everlasting are crowned.
Shout the glad tidings, etc.

3 Mortals, your homage be gratefully bringing,
And sweet let the gladsome hosanna arise ;
Ye angels, the full hallelujah be singing ;
One chorus resound through the earth and the skies.
Shout the glad tidings, etc.

Rev. William Augustus Muhlenburg. (1796—.) 1823

I HEAR THY WELCOME VOICE.

From "Hallowed Songs,"
By permission.

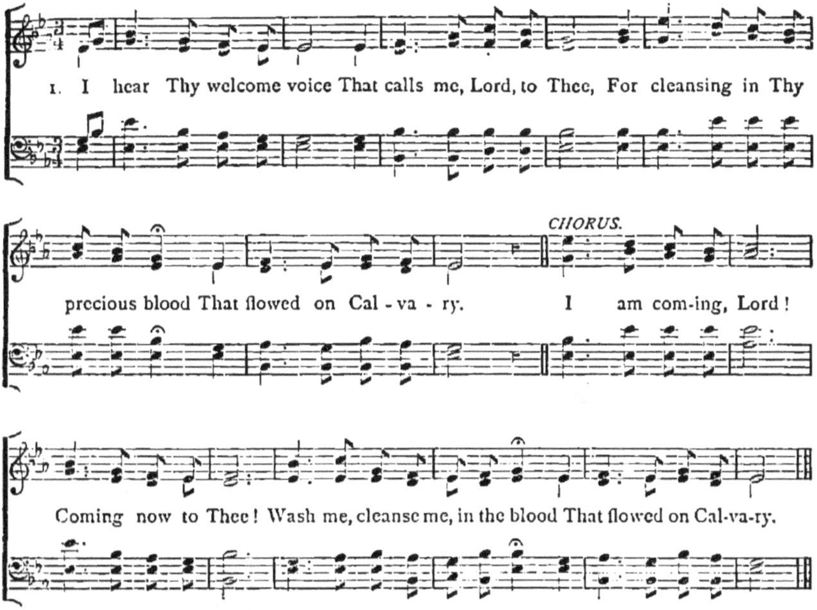

1. I hear Thy welcome voice That calls me, Lord, to Thee, For cleansing in Thy
precious blood That flowed on Cal - va - ry.
CHORUS.
I am com-ing, Lord!
Coming now to Thee! Wash me, cleanse me, in the blood That flowed on Cal-va-ry.

330 *"Come unto Me, all ye that labor and are heavy-laden, and I will give you rest."*—MATT. 11 : 28.

2 Though coming weak and vile,
Thou dost my strength assure;
Thou dost my vileness fully cleanse,
Till spotless all and pure.

3 'Tis Jesus calls me on
To perfect faith and love,
To perfect hope, and peace, and trust,
For earth and heaven above.

4 'Tis Jesus who confirms
The blessed work within,
By adding grace to welcomed grace,
Where reigned the power of sin.

5 And He the witness gives
To loyal hearts and free,
That every promise is fulfilled,
If faith but brings the plea.

6 All hail, atoning blood!
All hail, redeeming grace!
All hail, the Gift of Christ, our Lord,
Our Strength and Righteousness!

Rev. L. Hartsough.

WONDROUS LOVE.

William G. Fischer. By permission.

1. God lov'd the world of sin - ners lost And ruined by the fall; Sal-va - tion full, at
high - est cost, He of - fers free to all.
CHORUS.
Oh, 'twas love, 'twas wondrous love! The
love of God to me; It brought my Saviour from a-bove, To die on Cal - va - ry.

331 *"God so loved the world."*—JOHN 3 : 16.

2 E'en now by faith I claim Him mine,
The risen Son of God;
Redemption by His death I find,
And cleansing through the blood.

CHO. Oh, 'twas love, &c.

3 Love brings the glorious fullness in,
And to His saints makes known
The blessed rest from inbred sin,
Through faith in Christ alone.

CHO. Oh, 'twas love, &c.

4 Believing souls, rejoicing go;
There shall to you be given
A glorious foretaste, here below,
Of endless life in heaven.

CHO. Oh, 'twas love, &c.

5 Of victory now o'er Satan's power
Let all the ransomed sing,
And triumph in the dying hour
Through Christ the Lord our King.

CHO. Oh, 'twas love, &c.

Mrs. M. Stockton.

HOME OF THE SOUL. 145

From "Hallowed Songs." By permission.

1. I will sing you a song of that beau-ti-ful land, The far a-way
home of the soul, Where no storms ev-er beat on the glit-tering strand, While the
years of e-ter-ni-ty roll, While the years of e-ter-ni-ty roll; Where no
storms ev-er beat on the glit-tering strand, While the years of e-ter-ni-ty roll.

"*In my Father's house are many mansions.*"—JOHN 14:2.

2 Oh, that home of the soul, in my visions and dreams,
Its bright, jasper walls I can see;
Till I fancy but thinly the veil intervenes
|: Between the fair city and me. :| Till I fancy, etc.

3 That unchangable home is for you and for me,
Where Jesus of Nazareth stands;
The King of all kingdoms forever is He,
|: And He holdeth our crowns in His hands. :| The King of, etc.

4 Oh, how sweet it will be in that beautiful land,
So free from all sorrow and pain;
With songs on our lips and harps in our hands
|: To meet one another again. :| With songs on, etc.

Mrs. Ellen H. Gates.

WHAT HAST THOU DONE FOR ME?

146

P. P. Bliss. By permission.

Moderato.
1. I gave My life for thee, My precious blood I shed, That thou might'st ransom'd
be,.... And quickened from the dead; I gave, I gave My life for thee, What
hast thou giv'n for Me? I gave, I gave My life for thee, What hast thou giv'n for Me?

333

"*So Christ was once offered to bear the sins of many.*"—HEB. 9:28.

2 My Father's house of light,—
My glory-circled throne—
I left for earthly night,
For wand'rings sad and lone;
I left, I left it all for thee,
Hast thou left aught for Me?

3 I suffered much for thee,
More than thy tongue can tell,
Of bitterest agony,
To rescue thee from hell
I've borne, I've borne it all for thee,
What hast thou borne for Me?

4 And I have brought to thee,
Down from My home above,
Salvation full and free,
My pardon and My love;
I bring, I bring rich gifts to thee,
What hast thou brought to Me?

Miss Frances R. Havergal.

THE GATE AJAR FOR ME. 147

From "Hallowed Songs," By permission.

1. There is a gate that stands a-jar, And thro' its portals gleaming, A radiance from the
Cross a-far, The Saviour's love re-veal-ing.
REFRAIN.
Oh, depth of mer-cy! can it be That
gate was left a-jar for me? For me,.. for me?.. Was left a-jar for me?
For me, for me?

334 "*The gates of it shall not be shut at all by day: for there shall be no night there.*"—REV. 21 : 25.

2 That gate ajar stands free for all
Who seek through it salvation;
The rich and poor, the great and small,
Of every tribe and nation.

REF. Oh, depth of mercy! can it be
That gate was left ajar for me?

3 Press onward then, though foes may frown,
While mercy's gate is open;
Accept the cross, and win the crown,
Love's everlasting token.

REF. Oh, depth of mercy! can it be
That gate was left ajar for me?

4 Beyond the river's brink we'll lay
The cross that here is given,
And bear the crown of life away,
And love Him more in heaven.

REF. Oh, depth of mercy! can it be
That gate was left ajar for me?

Mrs. Lydia Bax

JESUS OF NAZARETH PASSETH BY.

148

Theo. E. Perkins. By permission.

1. What means this eager, anxious throng, Which moves with busy haste along—These wondrous gatherings
day by day? What means this strange commotion, pray? In accents hush'd the throng reply: "Je-sus of
Nazareth passeth by." In accents hush'd the throng reply: "Jesus of Nazareth passeth by."

335

"*He heard that it was Jesus of Nazareth.*"—Mark 13 : 47.

2 Who is this Jesus? Why should He
The city move so mightily?
A passing stranger, has He skill
To move the multitude at will?
Again the stirring notes reply:
"Jesus of Nazareth passeth by."

3 Jesus! 'tis He who once below
Man's pathway trod, 'mid pain and woe;
And burden'd ones, where'er He came,
Bro't out the sick, and deaf, and lame.
The blind rejoiced to hear the cry:
"Jesus of Nazareth passeth by."

4 Again He comes! From place to place
His holy footprints we can trace.
He pauseth at our threshold—nay,
He enters—condescends to stay.
Shall we not gladly raise the cry—
"Jesus of Nazareth passeth by?"

5 Ho! all ye heavy-laden, come!
Here's pardon, comfort, rest, and home;
Ye wanderers from a Father's face,
Return, accept His proffered grace.
Ye tempted ones, there's refuge nigh,
"Jesus of Nazareth passeth by."

6 But if you still this call refuse,
And all His wondrous love abuse,
Soon will He sadly from you turn,
Your bitter prayer for pardon spurn.
"Too late! too late!" will be the cry—
"Jesus of Nazareth *has passed by*."

Miss Eva Campbell.

I NEED THEE EVERY HOUR. 149

Rev. Robert Lowry. By permission.

1. I need Thee ev - ery hour, Most gra - cious Lord ; No ten - der voice like
Thine Can peace af - ford.
REFRAIN.
I need Thee, oh ! I need Thee ; Ev - ery hour I
need Thee ; O bless me now, my Sav - iour ! I come to Thee.

336

" *Without Me you can do nothing.*"—JOHN 15 : 5.

2 I need Thee every hour ;
Stay Thou near by ;
Temptations lose their power
When Thou art nigh.
REF.—I need Thee, etc.

3 I need Thee every hour,
In joy or pain ;
Come quickly and abide,
Or life is vain.
REF.—I need Thee, etc.

4 I need Thee every hour ;
Teach me Thy will ;
And Thy rich promises
In me fulfill.
REF.—I need Thee, etc.

5 I need Thee every hour,
Most Holy One ;
Oh, make me Thine indeed,
Thou blessed Son.
REF.—I need Thee, etc.

Mrs. Annie S. Hawks.

TRUSTING JESUS. **150** Wm. H. Doane. By permission.

1. Sim-ply trusting all the way, Taking Je - sus at His word; Simply trusting, when I
pray, Ev-ery prom-ise of my Lord. REFRAIN. Sim-ply trusting, sim-ply trusting, Trusting
Je - sus, that is all; To the cross of Christ I cling, Sim-ply trusting, that is all.

337

"I trust in Thee."—PSA. 25 : 2.

2 Trusting when my sky is bright,
Trusting when my heart is glad;
Trusting in the gloom of night,
When my every thought is sad.
REF.—Simply trusting, etc.

3 Trusting when 'tis well with me,
Trusting whatsoe'er befall;
Trusting Jesus' love for me,
Simply trusting, that is all.
REF.—Simply trusting, etc.

4 Trusting, tho' my strength may fail,
Trusting when the light is dim;
Trusting till within the vale,
I shall anchor safe within.
REF.—Simply trusting, etc.

4 Trusting when my sky is bright,
Trusting when the clouds descend;
Trusting in the gloom of night—
Simply trusting to the end.
REF.—Simply trusting, etc.

F. J. C.

CHRIST, THE LORD, IS RISEN. 151

Chester G. Allen.

GIRLS.
CHORUS.
GIRLS.
1. Christ, the Lord, is risen to-day, He is risen in - deed ; Christ, the Lord, is risen to-day,
CHORUS.
FULL CHORUS.
He is risen indeed ; "He captive led cap-tiv - i - ty, He robb'd the grave of vic- to- ry,"
He broke the bars of death, He broke the bars of death. Hallelu-jah, hal-le - lu - jah, hal-le-
lu - jah, A - men ; Hal-le - lu - jah, hal - le - lu - jah, hal- le - lu - jah, A - men.

338

"*He is risen.*"—MATT. 28 : 6.

2 Christ, the Lord, is risen, etc.
Let every mourning soul rejoice,
And sing with one united voice,
The Saviour rose to-day,
The Saviour rose to-day.
Hallelujah, etc.

3 Christ, the Lord, is risen, etc.
The great and glorious work is done,
Free grace to all thro' Christ, the Son;
Hosanna to His name,
Hosanna to His name.
Hallelujah, etc.

4 Christ, the Lord, is risen, etc.
Let all that fill the earth and sea
Break forth in tuneful melody,
And swell the mighty song,
And swell the mighty song.
Hallelujah, etc.

Fanny J. Crosby.

CHANTS.

Gregorian. Arr. by Thomas Tallis.
(1529—1585.) 1565.

SELECTION, No. 1. Ps. i.

1 BLESSED is the man that walketh not in the counsel | of the · · un- | godly, ‖ Nor
standeth in the way of sinners, nor sitteth in the | seat — | of the | scornful.
2 But his delight is in the | law · · of the | Lord; ‖ And in His law doth he | medi-
tate | day and | night.
3 And he shall be like a tree planted by the | rivers · · of | water, ‖ That bringeth
forth his | fruit — | in his | season;
4 His leaf also | shall not | wither; ‖ And whatso- | ever · · he | doeth · · shall | pros-
per.
5 The ungodly | are not | so: ‖ But are like the chaff which the | wind — | driveth
· · a- | way.
6 Therefore the ungodly shall not | stand · · in the | judgment, ‖ Nor sinners in the
congre- | gation | of the | righteous.
7 For the Lord knoweth the | way · · of the | righteous: ‖ But the way of the un- |
godly | shall — | perish.

SELECTION, No. 2. Ps. xxiii.

1 THE Lord is my Shepherd; I | shall not | want. ‖ He maketh me to lie down in
green pastures; He leadeth me beside the | still — | waters.
2 He restoreth my soul; He leadeth me in paths of righteousness for His | Name's
— | sake. ‖ Yea, though I walk through the valley of the shadow of death, I
will fear no evil: for Thou art with me; Thy rod and Thy staff | they — |
comfort me.
3 Thou preparest a table before me in the presence of mine enemies, Thou anointest
my head with oil; my | cup · · runneth | over. ‖ Surely goodness and mercy
shall follow me all the days of my life; and I will dwell in the house of the |
Lord, for | ever. ‖ A- | men.

153

Richard Farrant. (1536—1581.) 1570.

SELECTION, No. 3. Ps. lxvii.

1 God be merciful unto | us, and | bless us ; ‖ And show us the light of His countenance, and be | merci· ·ful | unto | us.

2 That Thy way may be known up | on — | earth ; ‖ Thy saving | health a- | mong all | nations.

3 Let the people praise Thee, | O — | God. ‖ Yea, let | all the· ·people | praise — | Thee.

4 O let the nations rejoice | and be | glad ; ‖ For Thou shalt judge the people righteously, and govern the | na· ·tions | upon | earth.

5 Let the people praise Thee, | O — | God ; ‖ Yea, let all the | people | praise — | Thee.

6 Then shall the earth bring | forth her | increase ; ‖ And God, even our own | God shall | give us· ·His | blessing.

7 God shall | bless — | us ; ‖ And all the ends of the | world shall | fear — | Him.

8 Glory be to the Father, and | to the | Son, ‖ And | to the | Holy | Ghost ;

9 As it was in the beginning, is now, and | ever | shall be, ‖ World | without | end. A- | men.

SELECTION, No. 4. Ps. xcii.

1 It is a good thing to give thanks un- | to the | Lord ; ‖ And to sing praises unto Thy | name — | O most | Highest.

2 To tell of Thy loving-kindness | early· ·in the | morning ; ‖ And of Thy | truth· ·in the | night — | season.

3 Upon an instrument of ten strings, and up- | on the | lute ; ‖ Upon a loud instrument, | and up- | on the | harp.

4 For Thou, Lord, hast made me glad | through Thy | works ; ‖ And I will rejoice in giving praise for the ope- | ration | of Thy | hands.

5 Glory be the Father, and | to the | Son, ‖ And | to the | Holy | Ghost ;

6 As it was in the beginning, is now, and | ever | shall be, ‖ World | without | end. A- | men.

Gregorian.

SELECTION, No. 5. Ps. c.

1 Make a joyful noise unto the Lord, | all ye | lands ‖ Serve the Lord with gladness; come before His | presence | with — | singing.
2 Know ye that the Lord | He is | God ‖ It is He that hath made us, and not we ourselves; we are His people, | and the | sheep of · · His | pasture.
3 Enter into His gates with thanksgiving, and into His | courts with | praise ‖ Be thankful unto Him, | and — | bless His | name.
4 For the Lord is good; His mercy is | ever- | lasting ‖ And His truth endureth to | all — | gene- | rations.

Gregorian 1st Tone. Harmonized by Thomas Tallis. (1529—1595.)

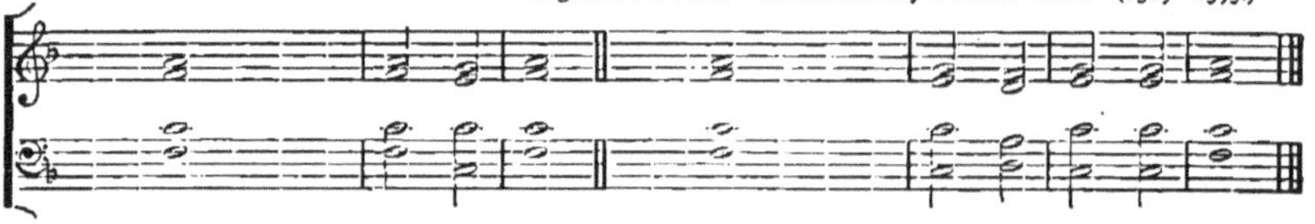

SELECTION, No. 6. Ps. li.

1 Have mercy upon me, O God, according to Thy | loving- | kindness: ‖ According unto the multitude of Thy tender mercies | blot out | my trans- | gressions.
2 Wash me thoroughly from | mine in- | iquity, ‖ And | cleanse me | from my | sin.
3 For I acknowledge | my trans- | gressions: ‖ And my | sin is | ever · · be- | fore me.
4 Hide Thy face | from my | sins, ‖ And blot out | all — | mine in- | iquities.
5 Create in me a clean | heart, O | God; ‖ And renew a right | spirit · · with- | in — | me.
6 Cast me not away | from Thy | presence; ‖ And take not Thy | Holy | Spirit | from me.
7 Restore unto me the joy of | Thy sal- | vation; ‖ And uphold me | with Thy | free — | Spirit.
8 Then will I teach trans- | gressors · · Thy | ways; ‖ And sinners shall be con- | verted | unto | Thee.
9 Deliver me from blood-guiltiness, O God, thou God of | my sal- | vation: ‖ And my tongue shall sing aloud | of Thy | righteous- | ness.
10 O Lord, open | Thou my | lips: ‖ And my mouth shall | shew forth | Thy — praise.
11 For Thou desirest not sacrifice; | else · · would I | give it: ‖ Thou delightest | not in | burnt — | offering.
12 The sacrifices of God are a | broken | spirit: ‖ A broken and contrite heart, O God, | Thou wilt | not de- | spise.

William Turner. (1651—1740.)

SELECTION, No. 7.

Ps. xlii.

1 As the hart panteth after the | water | brooks, ‖ So panteth my soul after | Thee, — | O — | God.

2 My soul thirsteth for God, for the | living | God! ‖ When shall I come and ap- | pear be- | fore — | God!

3 My tears have been my meat | day and | night, ‖ While they continually say unto me, | where is | thy — | God?

4 When I re- | member these | things, ‖ I pour | out my | soul — | in me;

5 For I had gone with the multitude, I went with them to the | house of | God, ‖ With the voice of joy and praise, with a multitude that | kept — | holy- | day.

6 Why art thou cast down, | O my | soul? ‖ And why are thou dis- | quiet- | ed in | me?

7 Hope | thou in | God: ‖ For I shall yet praise Him for the | help of | His — | countenance.

8 O send out Thy light and Thy truth: | let them | lead me; ‖ Let them bring me unto Thy holy hill, and | to Thy | taber - na - | cles.

9 Then will I go unto the altar of God, unto God my ex- | ceeding | joy: ‖ Yea, upon the harp will I praise | Thee, O | God, my | God.

10 Why art thou cast down, | O my | soul? ‖ And why art thou dis- | quiet- | ed with- | in me?

11 Hope | thou in — | God: ‖ For I shall yet praise Him, who is the health of my | countenance, | and my | God.

Richard Farrant. (1536—1581.) 1570.

SELECTION, No. 8.

Luke i. 68–71.

1 BLESSED be the Lord | God of | Israel, ‖ For He hath visited | and re- | deemed His | people;

2 And hath raised up a horn of sal- | vation | for us, ‖ In the house | of His | servant | David;

3 As He spake by the mouth of His | holy | prophets, ‖ Which have been | since the | world be- | gan;

4 That we should be saved | from our | enemies, ‖ And from the | hand of | all that | hate us,

Glory be to the Father, &c.

SELECTION, No. 9. Ps. xlvi.

1 GOD is our | refuge··and | strength, ‖ A very | present | help in | trouble.

2 Therefore will not we fear, though the | earth be | removed, ‖ And though the mountains be carried | into··the | midst··of the | sea.

3 Though the waters thereof | roar··and be | troubled, ‖ Though the mountains | shake··with the | swelling··there- | of.

4 There is a river, the streams whereof shall make glad the | city of | God, ‖ The holy place of the tabernacles | of the | Most — | High.

5 God is in the midst of her; she | shall··not be | moved: ‖ God shall | help her, and | that right | early.

6 The heathen raged, the | kingdoms··were | moved: ‖ He uttered His | voice, the | earth — | melted.

7 The Lord of | Hosts is | with us; ‖ The God of | Jacob | is our | refuge.

Glory be to the Father, and | to the | Son, ‖ And | to the | Holy | Ghost;

As it was in the beginning, is now, and | ever | shall be, ‖ World | without | end. A- | men.

Charles Norris. (1740—1790.)

SELECTION, No. 10. Ps. ciii.

1 PRAISE the Lord, | O my | soul; ‖ And all that is within me, | praise His | holy | name.

2 Praise the Lord, | O my | soul; ‖ And for- | get not | all His | benefits.

3 Who forgiveth | all thy | sin, ‖ And | healeth··all | thine in- | firmities.

4 Who saveth thy life | from de- | struction; ‖ And crowneth thee with | mercy ··and | loving- | kindness.

5 O praise the Lord, ye angels of His, ye that ex- | cel in | strength; ‖ Ye that fulfil His commandment, and hearken unto the | voice of | His — | word.

6 O praise the Lord, all | ye His | hosts; ‖ Ye servants of | His that | do His | pleasure.

*7 O speak good of the Lord, all ye works of His, in all places of | His do- | minion. ‖ Praise thou the | Lord, — | O my | soul.

SELECTION, No. 11. Ps. xcviii.

1 O SING unto the Lord a | new — | song; ‖ For | He hath · · done | marvel · · lous | things.
2 With His own right hand and with His | holy | arm, ‖ Hath He gotten Him- | self the | victo- | ry.
3 The Lord declared | His sal- | vation; ‖ His righteousness hath He openly | showed · · in the | sight · · of the | heathen.
4 He hath remembered His mercy and truth toward the | house of | Israel, ‖ And all the ends of the world have seen the sal- | vation | of our | God.
5 Show yourselves joyful unto the Lord, | all ye | lands; ‖ Sing, re- | joice, and | give — | thanks.
6 Praise the Lord up- | on the | harp; ‖ Sing to the Lord with a | psalm of | thanks- — | giving.
7 With trumpets | also · · and | shawms, ‖ O show yourselves joyful be- | fore the | Lord the | King.
8 Let the sea make a noise, and all that | therein | is; ‖ The round world, and | they that | dwell there- | in.
9 Let the floods clap their hands, and let the hills be joyful together be- | fore the | Lord; ‖ For He | cometh · · to | judge the | earth.
10 With righteousness shall He | judge the | world; ‖ And the | people | with — | equity.
Glory be to the Father, &c.

SELECTION, No. 12. Ps. xxiv.

1 THE earth is the Lord's, and the | fulness there- | of; ‖ The world and | they that | dwell there- | in.
2 For He hath founded it up- | on the | seas, ‖ And established | it up- | on the | floods.
3 Who shall ascend into the | hill · · of the | Lord? ‖ Or who shall stand | in His | holy | place?
4 He that hath clean hands, and a | pure — | heart; ‖ Who hath not lifted up his soul unto vanity, | nor — | sworn de- | ceitfully.
5 He shall receive the blessing | from the | Lord, ‖ And righteousness from the | God of | his sal- | vation.

6 This is the generation of | them that | seek Him, ‖ That | seek thy | face, O | Jacob.
7 Lift up your heads, O ye gates; and be ye lift up, ye ever- | lasting | doors; ‖ And the King of | glory | shall come | in.
8 Who is this | King of | glory? ‖ The Lord, strong and mighty, the | Lord — | mighty · · in | battle.
9 Lift up your heads, O ye gates; even lift them up, ye ever- | lasting | doors; ‖ And the King of | glory | shall come | in.
10 Who is this | King of | glory? ‖ The Lord of Hosts, | He is the | King of | glory.

William Boyce. (1710—1779.)

SELECTION, No. 13. Ps. xcv.

1 O COME, let us sing un- | to the | Lord; ‖ Let us heartily rejoice in the | strength of | our sal- | vation.
2 Let us come before His presence | with thanks- | giving; ‖ And show ourselves | glad in | Him with | psalms.
3 For the Lord is a | great — | God; ‖ And a great | King a- | bove all | gods.
4 In His hands are all the corners | of the | earth; ‖ And the strength of the | hills is | His — | also.
5 The sea is His | and He | made it; ‖ And His hands pre- | pared the | dry — | land.
6 O come, let us worship | and fall | down; ‖ And kneel be- | fore the | Lord our | Maker.
7 For He is the | Lord our | God; ‖ And we are the people of His pasture, and the | sheep of | His — | hand.
8 O worship the Lord in the | beauty of | holiness; ‖ Let the whole | earth · · stand in | awe of | Him.
*9 For He cometh, for He cometh to | judge the | earth; ‖ And with righteousness to judge the world, and the | people | with His | truth.
10 Glory be to the Father, and | to the | Son, ‖ And | to the | Holy | Ghost;
11 As it was in the beginning, is now, and | ever | shall be, ‖ World | without | end. A- | men.

SELECTION, No. 14. Ps. viii.

1 O LORD, our Lord, how excellent is Thy name in | all the | earth! ‖ Who hast set Thy | glory a- | bove the | heavens.
2 Out of the mouth of babes and sucklings hast Thou ordained strength be- | cause··of Thine | enemies, ‖ That Thou mightest still the | enemy | and the a- | venger.
3 When I consider Thy heavens, the | work of··Thy | fingers, ‖ The moon and the stars | which Thou | hast or- | dained;
4 What is man, that Thou art | mindful··of | him? ‖ And the son of man | that Thou | visitest | him?
5 For Thou hast made him a little lower | than the | angels, ‖ And hast crowned him with | glory | and — | honor.
6 Thou madest Him to have dominion over the | works··of Thy | hands; ‖ Thou hast put | all things | under··His | feet:
7 All | sheep and | oxen, ‖ Yea, and the | beasts — | of the | field;
8 The fowl of the air, and the | fish··of the | sea, ‖ And whatsoever passeth through the | paths — | of the | seas.
*8 O | Lord our | Lord, ‖ How excellent is Thy | name in | all the | earth.

SELECTION, No. 15. Ps. xix.

1 THE heavens declare the | glory··of | God; ‖ And the firmament | showeth··His | handy- | work.
2 Day unto day uttereth speech, and night unto | night showeth | knowledge. ‖ There is no speech nor language, where their | voice — | is not | heard.
3 Their line is gone out through | all the | earth, ‖ And their words to the | end — | of the | world.
4 In them hath He set a tabernacle | for the | sun, ‖ Which is as a bridegroom coming out of his chamber, and rejoiceth as a strong | man to | run a | race.
5 His going forth is from the end of the heaven, and his circuit unto the | ends — | of it; ‖ And there is nothing | hid··from the | heat there- | of.
6 The law of the Lord is perfect, con- | verting··the | soul: ‖ The testimony of the Lord is sure, | making | wise the | simple.

7 The statutes of the Lord are right, re- | joicing · · the | heart : ‖ The command-
ment of the Lord is | pure, en- | lightening · · the | eyes.
8 The fear of the Lord is clean, en- | during for | ever. ‖ The judgments of the
Lord are true and | righteous | alto- | gether.
9 More to be desired are they than gold, yea, than | much fine | gold : ‖ Sweeter
also than honey | and the | honey- | comb.
10 Moreover by them is Thy | servant | warned : ‖ And in keeping of them | there
is | great re- | ward.
11 Who can under- | stand his | errors ? ‖ Cleanse Thou | me from | secret | faults.
12 Keep back thy servant also from presumptuous sins ; let them not have do- |
minion | over me : ‖ Then shall I be upright, and I shall be innocent | from
the | great trans- | gression.
13* Let the words of my mouth, and the meditation of my heart, be acceptable | in
Thy | sight, ‖ O Lord, my | Strength, and | my Re- | deemer.

SELECTION, No. 16.

1 The mercy of the Lord is from everlasting to everlasting upon | them that |
fear Him, ‖ And His righteousness | unto | children's | children.
2 To such as | keep His | covenant ; ‖ And to those that remember His com- |
mandments · · to | do — | them.
3 He shall feed His | flock · · like a | shepherd : ‖ He shall gather the lambs with
His arm and | carry · · them | in His | bosom.
4 Suffer little children to come unto Me, and for- | bid them | not : ‖ For of | such
· · is the | kingdom · of | heaven.
5 For the promise is unto you, and | to your | children ; ‖ And to all that are afar
off, even as many as the | Lord our | God shall | call.
6 Then will I sprinkle clean | water · · up- | on you, ‖ And | ye shall | be — | clean :
7 A new heart also | will I | give you, ‖ And a new spirit | will I | put with- | in
you,
8 And I will take away the stony heart | out of · · your | flesh, ‖ And I will | give · ·
you a | heart of | flesh.
9 I will pour my Spirit up- | on thy | seed, ‖ And my | blessing · · up- | on thine |
offspring :
10 And they shall spring up as a- | mong the | grass, ‖ As | willows · · by the |
water- | courses.

GLORIA IN EXCELSIS. 161

1 Glory be to | God on | high, ‖ And on earth | peace, good- | will · · towards | men.
2 We praise Thee, we bless Thee, we | worship | Thee, ‖ We glorify Thee, we give thanks to | Thee for | Thy great | glory.

3 O Lord God, | heavenly | King, ‖ God the | Father | Al- — | mighty.
4 O Lord, the only begotten Son, | Jesus | Christ ; ‖ O Lord God, Lamb of | God, Son | of the | Father,

5 That takest away the | sins · · of the | world, ‖ Have mercy | upon | us.
6 Thou that takest away the | sins · · of the | world, ‖ Have mercy | upon | us.
7 Thou that takest away the | sins · · of the | world, ‖ Re- | ceive our | prayer.
8 Thou that sittest at the right hand of | God the | Father, ‖ Have mercy | upon | us.

9 For Thou | only · · art | holy : ‖ Thou | only | art the | Lord :
10 Thou only, O Christ, with the | Holy | Ghost, ‖ Art most high in the | glory · · of | God the | Father. ‖ A- | men.

INDEX OF TUNES.

INDEX OF CHANTS.

INDEX OF FIRST LINES.

INDEX OF SUBJECTS.

The Figures refer to the Numbers of the Hymns.

www.ingramcontent.com/pod-product-compliance
Lightning Source LLC
Chambersburg PA
CBHW020544270326
41927CB00006B/711